VICTORIAN FLOWERCRAFTS

VICTORIAN FLOWERCRAFTS

OVER 40 STYLISH GIFTS, DECORATIONS AND RECIPES

JANE NEWDICK

LITTLE, BROWN AND COMPANY
BOSTON · NEW YORK · TORONTO · LONDON

A LITTLE, BROWN BOOK

First published in Great Britain in 1994
by Little, Brown and Company

Conceived, designed and produced by Breslich & Foss
Golden House
28–31 Great Pulteney Street
London W1R 3DD

Typesetting, design and photography copyright © 1994 by Breslich & Foss
Text copyright © 1994 by Jane Newdick

Project Editor: Catriona Woodburn
Design: Nigel Partridge
Original Photography: Marie-Louise Avery
Styling for Original Photography: Jane Newdick

Breslich & Foss wish to thank Tom Woll for the idea for this book.

A CIP catalogue record for this book
is available from the British Library

ISBN 0-316-90736-7

10 9 8 7 6 5 4 3 2 1

Film origination by Dot Gradations, Essex, England
Printed and bound by Mandarin Offset Ltd., Hong Kong

Little, Brown and Company (UK) Ltd
Brettenham House
Lancaster Place
London WC2E 7EN

Contents

○　○　○

The Morning Room 6
PRESSED FERN STATIONERY 8, GIFT WRAPPING IDEAS 11, SWEET PEA ARRANGEMENTS 15,
ROSE WREATH 16, MINIATURE CORSAGES 18

○　○　○

The Pantry 20
SUGAR FLOWER DECORATIONS 23, CANDIED LILAC AND VIOLET FLOWERS 24, ROSE-PETAL HONEY 26,
TEAS AND TISANES 29, PAPER SHELF EDGING 31

○　○　○

The Kitchen 32
SALMAGUNDI 35, APRICOT SWEETMEATS 37, FRESH FLOWER DECORATIONS 38,
HERB-FLOWER CHEESES 43, HERB-FLOWER VINEGARS 45, WOODRUFF SUMMER CUP 47

○　○　○

The Bathroom And Linen Cupboard 48
SWEET SCENTING POWDER 50, MARIGOLD SKIN TONIC 53, ROSE AND OATMEAL SKIN SCRUB 56,
HERBAL HAIR RINSE 59, FLOWER-SCENTED SACHETS 60, VICTORIAN LAVENDER WATER 63

○　○　○

The Bedroom 64
STEPHANOTIS WEDDING BOUQUET 66, COLOGNE WATER 68, FABRIC ROSES 70, SPECIAL OCCASION POSIES 74,
VALENTINE POSY 77, DECORATED HAT 80, DRIED FLOWER MIXTURE 83

○　○　○

The Drawing Room 84
FLOWER SCRAP DECOUPAGE 87, SPATTERWORK LAMPSHADE 89, DRIED FLOWERS IN A FRAME 92,
DECOUPAGE BOX AND POTPOURRI 94, FLOWER-PETAL FRAME 96, DRIED FLOWER BALL 99

○　○　○

The Dining Room 100
NDIVIDUAL TABLE POSIES 102, FLOWER FINGER BOWLS 105, TABLE FLOWER DECORATION 106, IVY NAPKIN RINGS 109,
IVY AND ROSE TABLE DECORATION 111, FRUIT AND FLOWER CENTREPIECE 112, MENU AND PLACE CARDS 116

○　○　○

THE MORNING ROOM

THE VICTORIAN MORNING ROOM WAS USED IN THE MORNINGS,
MUCH LIKE A FAMILY ROOM AND FOR ALL KINDS OF DAYTIME
ACTIVITIES. POSITIONED TO CATCH THE MORNING LIGHT, IT WOULD
BE A PLACE FOR THE GIRLS IN THE HOUSEHOLD TO PURSUE A HOBBY
OR JUST TO CHATTER. THE LADY OF THE HOUSE MIGHT CHOOSE TO
WORK OUT THE DAY'S MENUS HERE AND WRITE A FEW LETTERS, OR
TALK TO THE HOUSEKEEPER ABOUT HOUSEHOLD MATTERS.
THE FURNISHINGS WOULD BE PRETTY AND FEMININE – LIGHTER AND
LESS STUFFY THAN THOSE OF THE RICHER AND MORE FORMAL
DRAWING AND DINING ROOMS.

*RIGHT: Morning light highlights a collection of gifts inspired by flowers.
Roses, sweet peas, ferns, and pelargoniums were all favourites of the
Victorian period, and here they decorate boxes, fill jugs and create
lavish garlands.*

PRESSED FERN STATIONERY

○　　○　　○

WHAT YOU WILL NEED: *Several Varieties of Fresh Ferns, Flower Press or Stack of Heavy Books, Blotting Paper, Loose Sheets of Writing Paper, Adhesive*

Ferns of all kinds were immensely popular in Victorian times. The whole subject of natural history, and in particular the study of botany, captured the imagination of people during this period. It was the heyday of the plant collector as well as the intrepid traveller, who could discover whole valleys of new plants and spectacular flowers in far-flung places. Back home, elaborate ferneries and grottoes were created from banks of soil and huge rocks, often complete with splashing water and large trees to offer shade. These were built in fashionable gardens and were home to large collections of the more hardy varieties of ferns, while the more tender tropical species and exotic tree ferns were grown under the cover of greenhouses.

RIGHT: After about a week, when the ferns are pressed and perfectly dry, glue them carefully to writing paper. Be sure the glue has thoroughly dried before folding your letter.

ABOVE: Spread out the fern leaves on large sheets of blotting paper. They should not overlap at all. Try different varieties to find which ones look best.

ABOVE: Cover the ferns with another sheet of blotting paper and make more layers of ferns and paper if you wish. Put them between large books with a weight on top.

Alongside collectors interested in cultivation, others scoured the countryside for wild species of ferns, bringing them home to press and display in elaborate and beautiful leather-bound albums, with each type carefully identified and labelled. The amateur study of botany became a common pastime, and some people even chose to specialize in a particular type of plant that they might dry, press, and then draw or paint in great detail. These days, collectors should only pick ferns from plants grown in a garden or from the many houseplant varieties.

The decorative shapes and leaf structure of ferns, and the fact that they are not very fleshy plants, make them particularly suitable for preserving; once pressed, they can be used for many different crafts. Because their leaf shapes were so attractive and they held a good outline when dry, ferns were regularly made into stencils and used as patterns for spatterwork designs (see page 89), and the fern motif itself was often included in fabric and wallpaper patterns of the day.

Fresh ferns were incorporated into bouquets and posies of flowers as green edging, and both fresh and dried ferns (such as the maidenhair variety) were used to garnish and decorate buffet foods and special desserts and cakes.

A simple single leaf of pressed fern glued to writing paper makes a stylish and unusual design. You could also try snipping off tiny parts of a pressed fern and gluing them all round the edge of a card as a border, or interspersing fronds of pressed fern among pressed flowers such as primroses or pansies for a more intricate design.

Pressing and drying the ferns takes a week or so, depending on the thickness of the leaves. If you have a special flower press, use it, but otherwise improvise with a stack of books and any solid, heavy objects placed on top. Blotting paper placed on both sides of the leaf works best to absorb moisture, but if this is difficult to obtain, you can use sheets of newspaper or any soft, unglazed type of paper. Check on the state of the leaf every few days. At one time people would leave drying leaves in layers of paper under a rug or heavy, loose carpet until they were ready, but this does not seem a very practical option these days, and in any case carpets are more likely to be fitted to the edges of the room.

The process of drying and pressing ferns can be repeated with many other kinds of plants. Choose leaves and flowers that are fairly flat and do not have bulky centres or stems. Suitable examples are pansies, violets and violas, primroses and hardy geraniums. Small sprigs of forget-me-not or cow parsley can be pressed complete, and they add a light, lacy effect when placed alongside more solid flower shapes. Beware of making fussy, over-elaborate pressed flower pictures and collages and instead use the flowers and leaves as elegantly and simply as possible – perhaps as a border or a few clustered together as a motif.

Use an adhesive that is designed for paper and that allows you a little time before it sets to arrange things or change the positions of your leaves on the surface. Preferably it should dry clear or at least enable you to remove any residue easily so that the finished effect is not spoiled.

GIFT WRAPPING IDEAS

○　　○　　○

WHAT YOU WILL NEED: *Plain Cream or Brown Wrapping-paper, Floral Print Wrapping-paper, Empty Gift Boxes, Hot-glue Gun or Wallpaper Adhesive, Plain Wide Satin Ribbon and/or Wire-edged Ribbon, Plain Luggage Labels and/or Gold-edged Cards, Dried Roses, Fresh Flowers and Foliage*

The plainest gift can be transformed by its presentation, and both fresh and dried flowers are extremely useful for turning simple presents into something rather more special. The beginnings of a commercial industry in printed greeting cards and papers had appeared in the mid-nineteenth century, but many people still took pride in handwriting their own messages and in parcelling up presents in boxes complete with string, sealing wax, and tie-on labels. Handmade greetings cards were often put together as a hobby, using scraps, silhouettes, tinsel, sequins, paper, lace, pressed flowers and ferns – and here good taste usually gave way to an exuberant style, which today we might consider verging on kitsch.

The first and most important rule to remember before wrapping a present is not to attempt to cover an odd or awkward-shaped object as it is. Always put an irregularly shaped present into a box first. This immediately provides a simple shape, and after only a little practice you should find it easy to fold paper around corners. Wrap the present in tissue paper first, to protect it, or lay it in a bed of shredded tissue.

If the box is attractive enough, it may only need the very simplest of embellishments – a beautiful

ABOVE: A bunch of brilliant pink dried roses can be the starting point for several very different gift wrapping ideas. Single dried roses, or rose petals, can be attached to wrapping or gift tags to give your present a special and individual touch.

bow or a spray of flowers – but you may wish to wrap the box first. You could use plain brown kraft paper (the type used for years to wrap parcels) or something more glamorous, whether home decorated or bought.

It is fun and satisfying to make simple printed patterns on plain paper with paint, either using little wooden blocks carved with motifs or the old-fashioned but inexpensive method of potato printing – cutting a raised design from the surface of the potato. Stencilling is another method of making a regular or random pattern on paper, or you could try spraying paint through cut-out shapes or even through paper doilies. The spatter technique is also appropriate (see page 89) or, if you have more courage, freehand stripes or checks painted with translucent watercolours on cream paper looks both smart and pretty.

Dried flowers and single, loose dried petals are useful for spot gluing onto finished wrapped presents, as long as the gift does not have to survive any subsequent rough handling, which might damage delicate flowers. A hot-glue gun is the simplest tool for attaching dried flowers to paper, but any suitable cold adhesive is fine, although slower, since you have to keep the flower in place until the glue has set.

ROUND BOX WITH ROSE PETALS
Cover a ready-made round box and lid with plain brown paper. If you use wallpaper adhesive, the paper will shrink tightly as it dries, and this will help to avoid wrinkles appearing on the surface.

Once the paper has dried thoroughly, split a dried rose into separate petals (care should be taken when splitting them to prevent their crumbling).

Glue the petals individually all over the box and lid. Finish off with a silky ribbon, tied into a bow.

PRINTED PAPER WITH DRIED ROSEBUD
This wrapping paper idea relies upon choosing a pretty floral gift paper as a starting point. The wrapping encloses a plain box containing the gift, while one perfect dried rosebud is glued to the top surface. Any floral wrapping-paper will work for this idea, and for a variation you could attach a tiny spray of dried flowers tied together with a ribbon.

ROSE ON CARD
A plain cream parchment paper is used to cover a shallow box, and a simple gold-edged card is glued to the top surface to make a name label. To decorate the label, make a small ribbon rose by rolling a short length of wire-edged ribbon round on itself and pinching it together at the base so that it looks like an open flower. To hold the rose in place, staple or sew a few stitches at the base (through all the thicknesses of the ribbon) and glue it on to the label.

RED RIBBON AND SPRAY OF FLOWERS
The box here is wrapped in plain cream paper to offset the lavishness of a deep cranberry-coloured wide satin ribbon. A simple knot, tied at the top with the ends left long and loose, is more effective here than a full-blown bow, as it leaves room to pin a small spray of fresh flowers behind it.

RIGHT: A soft satin ribbon makes a wonderful package decoration. The flowers used here are clove-scented dianthus and Sweet william.

SWEET PEA ARRANGEMENTS

○   ○   ○

WHAT YOU WILL NEED: *Sweet Peas in Mixed Colours, Various Glass Containers, such as a Cake Stand and Vase*

The scent of sweet peas filling a room is one of the greatest pleasures of summer. A Victorian morning room was just the place to find bowls full of deliciously scented flowers – freshly picked early in the day from the kitchen-garden borders – filling glass vases and special sweet pea dishes.

The sweet pea, as we know it these days, was only bred and developed from its original species in the late nineteenth century, while the frilly-petal form was not bred until early in the twentieth century. A version of the scented pea had been grown in gardens since 1700, but although it had a powerful perfume, it had inconspicuous blooms on weak stems and was available in only a small colour range. It took a Victorian gardener to realize the potential of the plant and develop it towards its modern form.

Sweet peas have universal appeal and are grown both by amateur gardeners and commercial growers for the cut-flower trade. Although they last only a few days as cut flowers, their pastel colours and scent make them enormously popular. Sweet peas have stiff straight stems, which makes arranging them easy, and no foliage on the stems to obscure the flowers. They generally look their best when arranged simply and not mixed with other flowers or

LEFT: This glorious profusion of sweet peas is massed in a sunny window so that the light shines through the coloured glass containers.

foliage. They look beautiful when isolated into separate colours, but equally ravishing when combined with other colours in careless profusion.

At one time, sweet peas were usually arranged in special holders, which were stood at the base of a vase or in a shallow bowl. These holders could consist of a series of metal spikes, which the stems were pushed into, or sometimes a series of holes, moulded from china or glass, into which the flower stems were pushed. Using one of these holders, the stems could be held away from each other to better display the flower heads. A more contemporary way to show off the blooms is to bunch the flowers together in a close mass, making a virtue of the flowers' textures and colours.

To make an elaborate, formal arrangement for a special occasion, you can create a Victorian-style tiered display by putting a short, trumpet-shaped glass vase in the centre of a glass cake stand and using both containers to arrange the flowers in different ways. For the top vase, simply bunch the flowers together and let them fan out gently; for the stand, cut the flower stems very short and lay the flowers all around the plate – having previously flooded the surface with enough water to cover the cut stems. If there is any danger of the vase becoming too top-heavy after it has been filled with flowers, then secure it firmly to the cake stand with small pieces of florist's tape. Always keep water levels topped off in containers filled with sweet peas, as the stems take up quite large amounts of liquid. Change the water every day to keep it fresh.

ROSE WREATH

o   o   o

WHAT YOU WILL NEED: *About 40 Old-fashioned Pink Roses, Sprigs of Honeysuckle, An Oasis-style Foam Wreath Base*

Through every major period of history the rose has been rediscovered and celebrated in some way. The Victorian period was no exception, and fresh roses found their way into gardens, conservatories, and houses; onto dresses; in hair decorations; and decking dining tables. As a motif the rose appeared on sprigged cotton prints as well as voluptuous woven fabrics, and it was printed onto wallpapers, included in paintings and trapped behind glaze on plates and dainty teacups.

The Victorians loved their roses large and full blown, fully petalled, and heavy as cabbages, with a heady scent if possible. In the garden they were trained to clamber up pergolas and arches, twine along ropes, and drape around chains bordering formal rose gardens. Moss roses, with their strange green mossy covering on bud and stem, were very much in fashion, and many new rose varieties were bred during this period and remain popular garden plants to this day.

To make a rose wreath for a summer day, you will need to be able to pick a basket of fresh blooms from your own garden or to choose the most natural types from a flower shop. Use an oasis-style foam base that can be soaked to hold water and provide the flower heads with constant moisture. Cut the rose stems quite short so that they can be pushed into the foam close enough to each other to make a

ABOVE AND RIGHT: Sumptuous, large-headed pink roses and sweet-smelling honeysuckle make a satisfyingly full and beautiful summer wreath to hang on a gate, door, or wall to welcome guests.

dense texture of petals. The colour scheme here is uncompromisingly pink, with no green foliage, but some sprigs of honeysuckle tucked here and there provide extra scent and a contrast in form to the round multipetalled roses. Included in this rose wreath are many old-fashioned varieties, such as 'Charles de Mills' and 'Fantin Latour'.

MINIATURE CORSAGES

○   ○   ○

WHAT YOU WILL NEED: *Small Fresh Flowers, Small Pieces of Foliage, Florist's Tape, Fine Wire, Scissors*

ABOVE: Reminiscent of a Victorian Valentine posy, this delicate mixture of pink flowers includes a rosebud and airy sprays of tiny-flowered London pride.

Flower sellers, positioned near offices and station entrances, were a common sight on the streets of Victorian London. Very often they sold tiny bunches of flowers that were meant for pinning to a dress or jacket as a decorative boutonnière. Single blooms were sold as "coat flowers", to be threaded through a buttonhole or attached to a lapel.

It seems unclear just when and how the adoption of boutonnières began, though they may be a derivation of the posies of flowers and herbs people once wore in the belief that the scent would protect them from diseases and foul air.

Smartly dressed men would always purchase a bloom to wear fresh each day. A small glass vial filled with water kept the bloom fresh. The stem of a flower was pushed through the buttonhole from the front, into a vial that was kept in a special small pocket inside the jacket. Scented flowers were the most popular for this purpose, especially posies of sweet violets, which appeared in the spring, and roses or pinks, available in the summer. Garden owners, of course, could pluck their own rosebuds and pin them in place, and men living in the country had the opportunity to pick wildflowers from the roadside to thread through their buttonholes.

For Victorian evening occasions, such as balls, dances, concerts, and operas a more splendid corsage of exotic flowers was required: gardenias or camellias perhaps, or tea rose and jasmine.

A corsage was once the term used to describe the bodice of a woman's dress, but it came to refer to the flower sprays designed for pinning to the shoulder or front. As a custom, corsages have really dropped out of fashion now, although they are still made up by florists for special occasions.

Some flower decorations were made for specific purposes, such as for adorning elaborate hairstyles,

ABOVE: These three different, delicately-coloured flower sprays would look equally well tucked into a hat, a hairdo, or a buttonhole. The cut stems are bound in florist's tape to keep in the moisture, so they should stay fresh for several hours at least.

or for pinning right around the hem of a ball gown, or decorating the edge of a veil or train. A woman might have flowers attached to her clothes, worn in her hair, and carry a posy of flowers over her wrist (leaving her hands free for dancing, eating, playing the piano and other activities).

THREE BOUTONNIERES

The little flower boutonnières here are simple, using fresh garden flowers in soft colours, and can be used to attach to a dress or hat or to decorate a special cake or gift. No great skill is needed to put them together, but the right kind of florist's tape is required to wrap the stems tightly and keep the moisture in. Pale green tape is the best colour, as it gives the stems a natural look.

Begin with a piece of foliage as the background to the spray. The foliage should have a stem long enough to attach the flowers to it. Lay the flowers on top of this, spreading them out so that they all show clearly. Either put the flower arrangement together in your hands, pinching the stems between your fingertips or, if you find it easier, work with the flowers on a table. Now tie the stems all together with fine wire to hold everything securely – spiralling the wire right down the length of the stems. Take a length of florist's tape and, starting at the top, wind it down the wire-wrapped stems, overlapping it and pulling and stretching as you go. At the bottom, seal the ends and bring the tape back up the stem a little way.

The flowers used in the three boutonnières here are as follows (clockwise from top): (1) lavender, forget-me-not, species lilac, sweet pea and honey-suckle; (2) artemisia foliage, rose and London pride; (3) golden marjoram, veronica, scented pelargonium and dianthus.

THE PANTRY

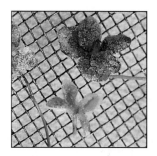

EVERY VICTORIAN HOUSE, BIG OR SMALL, REQUIRED A COOL STOREROOM FOR FOOD. WHILE GRAND HOUSES MIGHT HAVE HAD SPECIAL ROOMS FOR DIFFERENT PURPOSES, SUCH AS A DAIRY AND VEGETABLE STORE, THE PANTRY WAS AN ALL-PURPOSE PLACE, PERFECT FOR KEEPING A PIECE OF FINE CHEESE OR PIE FRESH. THE SHELVES WOULD CONTAIN ROWS OF PRESERVES, PICKLES AND JARS FILLED WITH GOOD THINGS FOR THE WINTER MONTHS. BESIDES THESE THERE MIGHT HAVE BEEN BASKETS OF EGGS OR A RICH FRUIT CAKE, AS WELL AS SPECIAL EXTRAS, SUCH AS CANDIED FLOWERS, FLAVOURED VINEGARS AND PACKETS OF SPECIAL TEAS.

RIGHT: A cool cupboard remains one of the best places for storing ingredients and keeping fresh those foods which are not placed in a refrigerator. Line shelves with clean paper, and decorate with small cut-out paper flowers.

SUGAR FLOWER DECORATIONS

○   ○   ○

WHAT YOU WILL NEED: *Sugar Paste for Moulding, Edible Natural Colours, Artificial Stamens, Stems, etc. (available from cake decorating and craft shops) or Ready-made Sugar-paste Decorations, Thin Ribbon*

The art of culinary presentation reached great heights during the Victorian period. Instructions for setting tables, folding linen, and decorating with flowers for dinner parties were common at a time when people were desperate to appear to be doing things in the correct way.

Cookbooks of the period were crammed with colour plates showing fabulously complicated desserts looking like pieces of sculpture or grand architecture rather than food. The sweet course of a meal provided the best opportunity for embellishment, but main dishes, particularly as part of a cold buffet, were just as richly decorated.

Our taste these days has greatly changed and we mostly prefer our food with a minimum of disguise or decoration. The only time when we still really decorate food is for a birthday, wedding, or some such special occasion. Iced cakes are part of a long tradition of celebratory food and we have come to expect that they should have flowers or icing or at least something to take them out of the ordinary.

Edible or inedible, decorations add to the pleasure of the food. Cake decorations made from sugar

LEFT: This light and ethereal decoration of spring primroses, made from pale yellow sugar paste, is suitable for birthday, wedding or other special occasion cakes.

ABOVE: A flower with a simple shape, such as this one, is the best kind to attempt if you are a beginner. For accuracy, copy your flower from a real bloom.

paste can be shaped into very realistic flowers. If you are unused to using it, then start with something very simple, such as this delicate spray of wild primroses.

The paste can be coloured, rolled, cut, and moulded into petals and flower forms. Take a real flower or a picture of a flower and copy its line and colours as accurately as possible. As the paste dries it hardens and remains so. Finish off this decoration by tying the stems together with thin ribbon.

CANDIED LILAC AND VIOLET FLOWERS

○ ○ ○

WHAT YOU WILL NEED: *Powdered Gum Arabic, Rose- or Orange-flower Water, Small Screw-top Jar, Fresh Violets, Fresh Lilac, Fine Sugar, Small Paintbrush, Tweezers*

Since medieval times, flowers have been preserved in many different ways to decorate and flavour foods and to make use of their medicinal and healing properties. Pickled rosebuds, for example, were used to enhance a winter vegetable dish, and tiny rose comfits (sugar-coated sweets containing a nut or seed) were taken to soothe sore throats and relieve the symptoms of a cold. Crystallized and

BELOW: The delicate process of painting each violet or lilac bloom and dipping it into the sugar is made easier with the right tools and a good light source.

candied flowers are probably the only remnants left of the tradition of these little sweet medicines, although flower-scented cachous and pastilles have long been popular as breath sweeteners and for aiding digestion.

Candied flowers can be scattered over puddings and fruit dishes or carefully arranged with other decoration on formal cakes and gâteaux, but they also make a delicious crisp addition to ice creams or any soft-textured creamy dessert. The Victorians were fond of a brown bread ice cream that was nearly always strewn with plenty of candied violets. (It is worth remembering that both violets and lilac combine well with chocolate, in looks and flavour.)

Before you begin to candy the flowers, you will need to mix up some gum arabic solution. This may take a couple of days to dissolve, so prepare it ahead of time and keep it stored ready for use in a small screw-top jar. Gum arabic is obtained from the acacia tree and is a sticky resinous substance used in many processes where an edible binder or glue is required. It is available from confectioners and cake decorating suppliers, pharmacies, and herbalists in powdered form. To make the solution, put a couple of spoonfuls of powdered gum arabic in a small jar and pour over enough rose- or orange-flower water to cover the powder. (Plain water can be used to make up the solution if no flower water is available.) Screw on the lid tightly and leave it to slowly dissolve, shaking it vigorously whenever you remember to do so. You should end up with a more or less clear, thick gum of a consistency that is brushable.

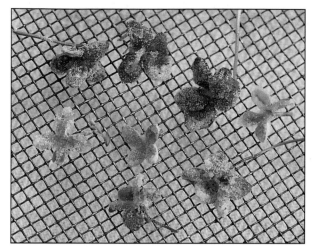

LEFT: The sugared flowers will take 12 hours or so to dry. Spread them out on a wire rack and leave them in a warm, airy room or near a gentle heat source.

BELOW: Elegant and unusual, the finished flowers are perfect decorations for delicate biscuits such as these. They also look good scattered over cakes or puddings.

Gum arabic will vary from batch to batch. Add a little more liquid if it seems too thick.

Once the solution is ready, collect some fresh violet and lilac flowers. Be sure that they are completely dry (place them on a tissue to absorb any excess moisture). In the case of lilac, you should pick the individual lilac florets off the stem, but for handling the violets it may be easier to leave a tiny piece of stem intact.

With a small brush, paint the gum solution all over the flowers, taking care not to leave any part of them unpainted. Now sprinkle sugar over them, or use the tweezers and dip the flowers into a shallow plate filled with sugar. You will find out which method is easiest as you do this – usually a combination of the two. Try to avoid attaching too much sugar or ending up with clumps of it on the petals. Now lay the sugared flowers onto a wire rack in a warm, airy place to dry. Leave them overnight; by morning they should be completely dry and crisp. Stored in an airtight container they will last several months.

ROSE PETAL HONEY

○   ○   ○

WHAT YOU WILL NEED: *Fresh, Strongly-scented Pink or Red Rose Petals, 15 oz (450 g) Mild-flavoured Honey, Food Processor, Small Jars with Lids*

Our ancestors weren't as wary as we are about eating flowers. They used petals and leaves from many species of plants as ingredients in, and additions to, recipes. These could add flavour and fragrance, as well as colour and texture.

The flavour of roses has long been popular, although these days its use is largely confined to sweet dishes. Distilled rose water is a wonderful flavouring to keep in the pantry, for it has a natural affinity with many fruits, fresh and dried, as well as with recipes with a Middle Eastern origin.

The Victorians had many delightful recipes for food incorporating fresh rose petals: rose-petal sorbet, rose-petal jelly and jam, and rose-petal butter. Teatime was the meal where these delicacies came into their own. Alongside tiny sandwiches with fillings like anchovy paste, egg and cress or cucumber would sit miniature triangles of bread with a filling of rose petals. The silver cake stands might have held tiny cakes and pastries decorated with crystallized petals, and the accompanying tea for such treats would have been an exotic, flowery mixture of petals and China tea.

The height of the rose season is in early summer, though of course roses can be bought all year round. Sadly, most of the commercially grown varieties are bred for their looks and length of stem, so that few have the magnificent scent and full-petalled luxury of real garden roses. If you would like to grow a suitable rose in your own garden, you could try the old rose, *Rosa gallica* var. *officinalis*, which was grown extensively in the past for its perfume and used to distil essential rose oil. Its flowers are a brilliant shocking pink. The following varieties are also good choices; they all have a good scent and range from pale pink to deep red: 'Crimson Glory', 'Souvenir du Dr Jamain', 'Louise Odier', 'Fantin Latour', 'Madame Isaac Pereire', and 'Souvenir de la Malmaison'.

To make rose-petal honey you will need a good quantity of fresh rose petals which have not had any insecticide or fungicide sprays put on them. The honey you use as a base should be very mild so that its flavor doesn't mask that of the rose. A good choice would be an acacia honey.

Pour 15 oz (450 g) of honey into a small pan and heat it very gently, until hot but not boiling. Put 4 cupfuls of clean, dry, fresh, highly scented rose petals into a food processor and shred them quite finely. Now pour the hot honey over the petals and process for a few seconds more. The petals will change colour in the heat. Now pour the rose honey into small jars and seal well. This will keep in a cool place for several months.

Use the honey in sandwiches or spread on cookies, scones or cakes. It is also delicious spooned over ice cream or stirred into plain yogurt.

RIGHT: This refined tea complements thin slices of bread and butter spread with rose petal honey.

TEAS AND TISANES

○   ○   ○

WHAT YOU WILL NEED: *Dried Orange Blossoms, China or other delicately-flavored Tea*

There has been a great revival in the art of tea-making and concocting drinks based on leaves, fruits, herbs and flowers. These tend to go under a general heading of 'tisanes' – which is the word the French use for a decoction of water and herbs. These delicious drinks have become popular again as many people move towards healthier eating and avoiding caffeine.

The Victorians were very fond of inventing all kinds of drinks for different occasions and it was necessary to have plenty of nonalcoholic choices. In summer, homemade refreshing drinks such as lemonade and barley water were very popular, although a constant problem was the quality of the water needed to make them. Tea at least was always safe because the water was boiled first. Indian and China teas were expensive for many people, but other kinds of 'teas' were popular.

Country people had recipes for infusions made from wild and garden plants, usually made for specific purposes such as clearing a bad head cold, soothing poor digestion, or easing childbirth. The Victorians brewed violet tea for coughs, lime flower tea for hysteria and chamomile tea for dyspepsia.

LEFT: This beautiful nineteenth-century wooden tea caddy is the perfect place to store your delicately flavoured, homemade orange blossom tea. In the foreground is a lime blossom tisane.

We still drink lime flower tea for its soothing effect and chamomile tea because it aids digestion and sound sleep.

The five o'clock tea-drinking ritual in grand houses was elaborate and, though both sexes were involved, these afternoon 'at homes' were very much the woman's domain. Unlike the homely family teas partaken in many households – when people simply gathered for a cup of tea, a simple fruit cake, and bread and butter – these events were quite lavish, with fairly sophisticated food.

The tea-making itself could be a complicated little ritual, with jugs and kettles of boiling water, silver spoons, beautiful wooden tea caddies, tea strainers, and little jugs of cream or milk to add. The thinnest porcelain was the most favoured material for tea cups, but every tea drinker was catered for, whether they used the finest china or thick earthenware mugs, by the great china factories that were at the height of their success in the nineteenth century.

ORANGE BLOSSOM TEA

To make orange blossom tea you simply need to mix a proportion of dried orange blossoms with dry tea leaves of your choice. These kinds of flower teas are best drunk without milk, so a delicate China tea such as a Keemun is preferable to a strong Indian tea with a lot of character. Try mixing 10 parts tea leaves to 1 part orange flowers, using whatever volume measure you choose. Make a batch of tea, taste it, and adjust the proportions to taste. Store the mixture in tins or paper bags.

PAPER SHELF EDGING

○   ○   ○

WHAT YOU WILL NEED: *White Paper Shelf Edging, Floral Wallpaper or Wrapping-paper, Paper Adhesive, Scissors*

The pantry, or larder, was a vitally important place in any Victorian household. It was here that much of the summer harvest of fruit and vegetables was preserved in various ways for the winter months. It would also hold stores of grain and flour and other dry goods, as well as eggs and any other ingredients that needed cool, airy surroundings.

It is unusual to find a new house built with a pantry. For foods that don't require the icy-cold of a refrigerator, most people have to make do with a few shelves in a kitchen cupboard. Here, paper shelf edging is a marvellous decorative idea that enlivens less interesting surfaces and adds a pretty and homely touch.

Collections of china and glass are enhanced by a backdrop of crisp white lacy paper. This version has small, paper flower cutouts attached all the way along it and is very simple to make. It could be the starting point for a more-complicated design matching a particular room scheme. If you cannot find a shelf paper with a lace edge like this one, then it is easy to cut strips off rectangular or scalloped paper doilies to fit and glue these at intervals along the edge of plain shelf paper.

LEFT: These beautiful roses, cut from a spare roll of wallpaper, and attached to a lacy paper border, freshen up a gloomy pantry space.

ABOVE: It can be satisfying to choose a motif that will match patterned china or perhaps echo the wallpaper in your kitchen or dining room.

To create the flower border, you will need to find a flower-printed wrapping-paper or wallpaper that has a repeated pattern. The alternative is to use reproduction Victorian paper scraps in a floral design. Cut out as many single flower shapes as you need and then work out where to space them along the shelf edge.

Cut the shelf paper to fit your space. Whether you start with one flower at either end, and work towards the centre, or start at one side and work across, be sure to allow equal spacing between flowers. Glue the flowers in place according to the depth of lace overhang on the shelf. Put the paper on the shelf and fold the front edge into place.

THE KITCHEN

FOR CENTURIES, FLOWERS HAVE BEEN BROUGHT INTO THE KITCHEN
FROM GARDENS AND HEDGEROWS, AND BEEN USED BOTH IN FOOD
AND AS EMBELLISHMENTS TO FINISHED DISHES. SADLY, WE ARE FAR
LESS CREATIVE AND AMBITIOUS THAN OUR ANCESTORS WERE IN
MAKING USE OF THEM.
THE VICTORIANS LOVED THEIR MEALS TO BE SERVED SURROUNDED BY
DISPLAYS OF FLOWERS, BOTH REAL AND ARTIFICIAL, AND THEIR
GREAT PASSION FOR EVERYTHING HORTICULTURAL SPILLED OVER
INTO THE FOOD THEY ATE – INFLUENCING FLAVOURS, ADDING SCENTS
AND ENHANCING COLOURS.

*RIGHT: Herb-flower vinegars in pretty glass bottles and decorated herb-flower
cheeses not only look wonderful, they also make delicious presents.
For serving the cheeses at a summer picnic, add petals and summer fruits
for eye-catching colour.*

SALMAGUNDI

○　　○　　○

WHAT YOU WILL NEED: *Fresh Baby Vegetables, such as Beets, Carrots, Green Beans, Snow Peas, Pickled Gherkins, Hard-boiled Eggs, Scallions, Cress, Fresh Flowers for Decoration, such as Violas, Pansies, Chive Flowers, Cornflower*

These days, salads are as colourful and varied in their ingredients as our imagination allows. We have an enormous choice of ingredients at hand at all times of year and inspiration from many cuisines and cultures.

In Victorian times, a varied salad was a popular accompaniment to many meals. Tomatoes were not considered suitable for eating raw, and so they were not included in salads until the very end of the Victorian period. Instead, colour was brought to salads with red-leafed lettuce varieties, beets, radishes, and a garnish of herbs or chopped egg.

A great salad dish of the period, called salmagundi, which was also extremely popular in the eighteenth century, was a set-piece dish from which people could choose the vegetables they preferred. The ingredients were laid out in glorious patterns of varying colours and shapes – either spread out fairly flat, encircling a mound of one particular ingredient, or layered in a crystal bowl. We still have some of these composed salads in modern recipe books, but the salad as a work of art has somewhat dropped from favour.

LEFT: This is a modern version of the Victorian salad known as salmagundi.

This version of salmagundi has egg, but no meat or fish, although the Victorian versions often had cold cooked chicken or beef and pickled or salted fish added for piquancy. They often contained some preserved ingredients, too, and an important element in a salmagundi was the final topping decoration of edible herbs and flowers, which added more varied tastes and colour.

Depending on the time of year, you can use all kinds of edible flowers and herbs. Late summer will provide your salad with marigold petals and nasturtium flowers, as well as the golden-yellow flowers of zucchini and the brilliant blue of star-shaped borage flowers, which make a lovely contrast to the green of the vegetables.

To compose the salad, begin by blanching very briefly those vegetables that need it and then refreshing them in cold water. Drain and dry them. Cook baby beets until they are tender, and leave them to cool. Separate the yolk and white from hard-boiled eggs and chop each very finely. Trim all the vegetables to roughly equal sizes. Wash and trim the scallions. Make a pattern with the chopped egg in the centre of a large shallow dish, before arranging the vegetables around it, creating patterns and areas of different colours. Use lines of green beans to separate different ingredients where necessary. Work in roughly concentric rings of ingredients until the plate is filled. Decorate with flowers and herb flowers. Serve the salmagundi immediately with a good vinaigrette or similar dressing (perhaps mixed with more chopped herbs and flowers).

APRICOT SWEETMEATS

○   ○   ○

WHAT YOU WILL NEED: *Whole or Ground Almonds, Candied Orange Peel, Scissors, Dried Apricots, Dried Dates, Fresh Orange Juice, Orange-Flower Water, Slivers of Blanched Almonds, Small Paper or Foil Baking Cups*

These exotic-tasting sweetmeats have a dash of the Middle East about them with their use of orange-flower water for flavouring. This is distilled from the highly scented blossoms of the orange tree and it has been used for centuries in cooking, as well as in cosmetics and perfumes. It is a useful natural flavouring to have in the cupboard, but it should be used sparingly for a subtle hint of flavour rather than an overwhelming one. It is particularly delicious when sprinkled over a dish of peeled and sliced oranges or clementines, and it also combines well with fresh fruit such as strawberries and pineapples. The flavour of dried fruit compotes for winter meals can also be enhanced if a little orange-flower water is added to their natural juices. You could also try adding a few drops to some grated orange zest and beating it into some fresh curd or cream cheese.

Apricots were a favourite Victorian fruit, grown under glass or against walls in sheltered kitchen

LEFT: These delicious sweetmeats made from dried apricots and other fruits take on an exotic air when served up in a golden box and decorated with fresh leaves.

gardens. It is rare to find a perfect fresh, ripe apricot that is good enough to eat raw; they often taste better when poached or cooked. Dried apricots, however, are consistently good and can be used in many different recipes. Although they look less appetizing, the ones with the most flavour are usually smaller and darker than the fat, orange, 'no need to soak' variety. These tend to have a sweetness lacking the tartness and depth of flavour that gives the true apricot taste.

For this recipe, a food processor will save hours of chopping with a knife. Grind whole almonds – either blanched or with the skins on – or, if you want to save time, buy them already ground. You can substitute other nuts such as pistachios or hazel nuts. Use candied orange peel that comes in whole pieces rather than the ready-chopped kind, which is often overly sweet and tasteless. The easiest way to cut up peel for the food processor is with scissors. Dip the scissors into hot water now and again to stop them getting stuck together.

Put the apricots, dates, ground almonds, candied peel, and orange juice in the food processor. Process until well blended. Add the orange-flower water, process briefly, and then taste, adding more if necessary. Now roll small pieces of the mixture into balls with your hands and put each one into a small paper or foil baking cup. Decorate the top of each with a sliver of almond, and allow them to dry off slightly in a cool, airy place before boxing up.

FRESH FLOWER DECORATIONS

○   ○   ○

WHAT YOU WILL NEED:

LEMON MOUSSE WITH JASMINE FLOWERS: 4 Large Eggs, 6 oz (175 g) Superfine Sugar, 2 Unwaxed Lemons, 5 fl oz (150 ml) Water, ¼ oz (15 g) Unflavoured Gelatin, Cream or Yogurt (optional), Fresh Jasmine

ROSE ANGEL CAKE: 1 oz (25 g) Plain Flour, 1 oz (25 g) Corn flour, 5 oz (150 g) Superfine Sugar, 5 Egg Whites, A Few Drops Pure Vanilla Extract, Confectioner's Sugar for Dusting, Kugelhof Ring Mould, Fresh Rose Heads

CHOCOLATE TRUFFLE CAKE WITH LILAC: 6½ oz (200 g) Dark Chocolate, Plus Extra for Icing, 3½ oz (100 g) Unsalted Butter, 2 Tablespoons Soft Brown Sugar, 4 Eggs, 2½ oz (75 g) Plain Flour, ½ Teaspoon Baking Powder, 1 Teaspoon Pure Vanilla Extract, Sour Cream, as Desired, for Icing, Fresh Lilac, Fern Sprigs

The food in the homes of wealthy Victorians was almost overwhelmed by its attendant decoration. Tiny vegetables were carved into special shapes, special skewers were threaded with strips of edible garnish and laid alongside platters, and sugar was spun into golden cages to enclose moulded desserts.

In comparison with the Victorians, our meals today are simple and quick. However, there are still times when we make a large cake to slice at table or individual bowls of a special mousse. These are the times to decorate with fresh flowers.

LEMON MOUSSE WITH JASMINE FLOWERS

The dessert course was the place in the meal where cooks could let loose their artistic talents. Huge, towering, creamy puddings and jellies moulded in turreted and crenellated shapes defied gravity amidst rows of fresh berries, piped cream, icing or sliced crystallized fruits. With all such edifices, flowers, both fresh and candied, were vitally important items to add some colour and softness to the finished masterpiece.

For this lemon mousse, first separate the eggs and add the sugar to the yolks. Grate the rind from one of the lemons and add this. Next, squeeze both lemons and add the strained lemon juice to the mixture before whisking it all together until well blended.

Put the water into a small pan and sprinkle the gelatin over it. Leave this to stand for a few minutes and then place the pan over very low heat until the gelatin has dissolved. Pour this in a thin stream from high over the bowl onto the egg and lemon mixture. Whisk again to combine everything thoroughly and then set aside to thicken.

Stiffly beat the egg whites in a separate bowl, then gently fold them into the thickening mixture. Pour the mousse into one large serving bowl and chill.

Top with thick yogurt or whipped cream or, for something light and refreshing, serve completely plain. Decorate with sprigs of fresh jasmine flowers and leaves.

RIGHT: This light-textured and delicate-tasting lemon mousse demands an attractive decoration that doesn't overshadow it. Fresh jasmine is perfect and, although it is not meant to be eaten in this dessert, it is edible.

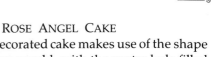

ABOVE: A plain and simple angel food cake can be turned into the most glamorous and Parisian of confections by simply placing a few exquisite – and preferably scented – fresh roses on the top.

RIGHT: Old-fashioned and indulgently rich, this chocolate truffle cake contrasts exquisitely with the pale mauve lilacs bordering it. Add a tiny bunch backed with a fern leaf and tied with a narrow ribbon to the top of the cake, and serve up with the family silver.

ROSE ANGEL CAKE

This idea for a decorated cake makes use of the shape of a kugelhof ring mould, with the centre hole filled with fresh pink roses. This is a plain angel food cake, but you could flavour it with a few drops of rose-water or even add chopped fresh rose petals.

Sift the flours and 1 oz (25 g) of the sugar together. Whisk the egg whites until they are very stiff, then add the remaining sugar to them, a spoonful at a time. Continue whisking until the consistency has thickened. Fold the whites into the flours and add the vanilla extract. Spoon the mixture into an 8-in (20-cm) round mould, and bake at 350°F (180°C/ Gas 4) for 35 to 40 minutes. Turn out onto a wire rack to cool, and sprinkle with confectioner's sugar. When cool, arrange whole pink rose heads in the centre.

CHOCOLATE TRUFFLE CAKE WITH LILAC

Use the best chocolate that you can afford – namely one with a high percentage of cocoa solids.

Melt the chocolate in a large saucepan. Beat the butter with half the sugar until light and fluffy. Separate the eggs and add the yolks one at a time to the mixture, beating well. Stir in the melted chocolate. Sift the flour and baking powder, and fold them into the mixture with a metal spoon. Beat the egg whites with the remaining sugar until stiff, then carefully fold this into the cake mixture along with the vanilla extract. Pour into a buttered and parchment-paper-lined loaf pan or an 8-in (20-cm) round springform pan and bake in the oven at 350°F (180°C/ Gas 4) for about 40 minutes. Leave to cool a little in the pan before turning it out onto a wire rack. Ice with a favourite chocolate icing, or chocolate melted with sour cream, and decorate by surrounding with fresh lilac heads and a small posy of lilac with fern leaf on top.

HERB-FLOWER CHEESES

○ ○ ○

WHAT YOU WILL NEED: *Fresh Cow's or Goat's Milk Cheese, Chive Flowers, Scented Geranium Leaves and Flowers, Other Herb Flowers, such as Thyme, Lavender, etc., Herb Leaves, such as Lovage, Sweet Cicely, Tarragon*

In the days before reliable methods of refrigerating food, keeping milk fresh was a problem. People devised all kinds of ways of keeping it cool in warm weather, with patent milk coolers and wet cloths. Most houses did at least have a cool kitchen or pantry in which to store dairy foods on stone, slate or marble shelves. When it was plentiful, surplus fresh milk was used for making butter and hard cheeses, but in the summer months, when milk turned sour more quickly, it was put to use making curd cheese.

To make curd cheese, the sour milk was placed in muslin or cheesecloth bags and hung up to drip overnight, turning into a delicious soft cheese and leaving a liquid whey. The curd cheese would be seasoned and flavoured – either to eat on its own, or used to make tarts and cheesecakes.

It is harder to achieve the same effect these days, as pasteurized milk does not sour naturally. Howver, there are plenty of commercially made fresh curd or other soft cheeses available today, so it is not necessary to make it from scratch. Once you have found a good source of cheese, you can add your own choice of flavourings.

You can roll soft cheese into a large single log shape and coat this with chopped herbs and flowers, or make several small, round, individual cheeses and then do the same.

If you would like a strong flavour running right through the body of the cheese, mix some very finely chopped fresh herbs into the cheese before shaping it. If your cheese is a little too soft and difficult to handle, wrap it in muslin and leave it to drain for a few hours, either by suspending it over a sieve or using a special cheese draining mould if you have one.

You can buy small china cheese moulds in different shapes. Another idea is to wrap complete cheeses in large herb leaves (such as sweet cicely or lovage leaves). Tie them up neatly, and leave them for a while for the flavour to penetrate the cheese slightly.

For other flavours, chive flowers make a pretty coating and can be used alone or with their leaves for a stronger taste. A little garlic also makes a pleasant addition. Sweet geranium flowers and leaves from rose- or lemon-scented varieties make a good choice for flavouring a cheese to eat with fruit.

Finely chop or shred about a teaspoonful of your chosen herb or flower to add to 4 oz (100 g) fresh cheese. If you like, you can add a little cream and stiffly beaten egg white to the flower-scented cheese, before draining it in individual heart-shaped moulds to make a variation of the French classic, *coeur à la crême.*

LEFT: A fine ending to a summer meal is a plate of different types of soft cheese, flavoured and scented with herbs and flowers. Sweet cicely, chives and scented geraniums are some of the choices.

HERB-FLOWER VINEGARS

o   o   o

WHAT YOU WILL NEED: *White Wine or Cider Vinegar, Elder flowers, Glass Bottles with Corks or Screw Tops*

Vinegars, both plain and flavoured, are now generally used in salad dressings and sauces and to add a dash of sharpness and flavour. At one time, however, flavoured vinegars were used for many different purposes. Diluted with water and sweetened, they became refreshing summer drinks; and raspberry or elderberry vinegar, in particular, were taken in teaspoonfuls to relieve the symptoms of colds and sore throats. They had other uses, too, in the bathroom, where they were diluted and used as a hair rinse or a refreshing bath additive. Floral vinegars were made up as skin tonics or toning lotions, and it makes sense to revive these old ideas since vinegar is naturally acidic and counteracts the drying effect of soaps, shampoos and cleansers.

In *Beeton's Book of Household Management*, Mrs Beeton gives recipes for chili, celery, gooseberry, cucumber, horseradish and mint vinegar, but today we are likely to choose red and white wine or cider vinegars for dressings and general culinary use and reserve luxurious vinegars, such as champagne and sherry, for special recipes where the flavour will be noticed. A dash of vinegar disguises the fact that you have reduced the salt in a recipe, and vinegar is also a vital ingredient in a marinade for tenderizing meat. A bottle of flavoured vinegar in the kitchen is as useful as a lemon for adding piquancy and sharpness.

Hundreds of flavours can be added to vinegars, many of the most successful being herbs, flowers and spices. You might like to try something straightforward like chives and chive flowers, but if you are inclined to experiment, then this is certainly an area in which there is still much to discover.

The easiest method of flavouring vinegar is to use it cold and let the flavourings steep in it slowly. To speed up the process a little, however, the vinegar can be heated first and then poured on to the ingredients. Any fresh green foliage will, of course, rapidly lose its colour this way, but it does this in time anyway with the cold method. If you plan to give the vinegar away as a gift, it is a good idea to take out the first lot of herbs or flowers and replace them with fresh ones before finally sealing the bottle.

Flavoured vinegars should keep well in a cool, dark place for many months. Elder flower vinegar is an unusual and delicious variety to add to your vinegar repertoire. It is easily made, but only in mid-summer when the elder tree is in bloom. Pick bunches of the flowers on a dry day and shake out any tiny insects. Avoid washing the flowers if possible, as they are difficult to dry afterward. Fill a jar or bottle with cider vinegar and pop in two or three flower heads. Cork or seal the bottle and leave it for about three weeks, shaking it occasionally. Finally, strain off the vinegar when the flavour is strong enough.

RIGHT: Just one variety of the many different flower- and herb-flavoured vinegars it is possible to make. This one has the subtle muscat flavour of elder flower from a summer hedgerow.

WOODRUFF SUMMER CUP

○   ○   ○

WHAT YOU WILL NEED: *Handful of Sweet Woodruff, 2 Teaspoons of China Tea, ½ lb (250 g) Strawberries, 40 fl oz (1.2 l) Pure Apple Juice, 1 Lemon, 1 Orange, Ice, Mineral Water (optional), Woodruff for Decoration*

When reading the recipes for drinks from Victorian times, one gets the impression of a constant whirl of dances and parties, suppers and musical evenings, croquet games and summer fetes. These may have been the pastimes of a few wealthy and sociable people, but the working people in the town or countryside also had their entertainments, which were accompanied by a vast range of seasonal drinks. The heat of hay making and summer fieldwork meant that gallons of barley water, ale and cold tea were drunk to quench the workers' thirsts, and children enjoyed lemonade and ginger beer. All kinds of other brews were made, including country-flower or fruit wines and nettle, dandelion or hop beer.

Indoors during the winter months there were many recipes for hot punches and caudles, possets and neguses. On summer days, mixed cups took over. These might be based on champagne or claret or could be nonalcoholic, with a base of tea or lemonade. These delicate mixtures were designed to refresh the drinker and were usually sparkled with ice or sugar crystals and decorated with strawberries or other colourful summer fruits, herbs, and flowers, such as lemon balm and borage.

Old recipes make much use of the flavours of flowers such as sweet woodruff, and there is a very ancient European recipe for a drink, made from this pretty woodland and garden flower, to be drunk on feast days at the beginning of summer. Borage was also a favourite for a summer claret cup, where it imparted its faint cucumber taste and the aroma from its leaves to the liquid. The brilliant blue flowers were scattered over the surface as a decoration. Mint has always been used to add its cool, refreshing scent, and there are many recipes for mint-based cups from the New and Old Worlds. The woodruff used here gives a very special flavour and the little flowers look pretty floating in the punch bowl.

Put a handful of fresh or dried woodruff in a jug and pour 10 fl oz (300 ml) of boiling water over it. Leave to infuse. In the meantime, brew the China tea, strain 10 fl oz (300 ml) of it and leave it to cool. Slice the strawberries and put them in a large bowl. Add chilled apple juice, then the cold tea and strained herb infusion and the strained, squeezed juice of one lemon and one orange. Add ice cubes, taste, and dilute with a little mineral water, still or sparkling, if needed. Scatter fresh woodruff flowers on the surface and serve very cold.

LEFT: This wonderfully refreshing summer cup is flavoured with sweet woodruff and brilliant scarlet strawberries. Serve it in place of afternoon tea, using a plain white china or clear glass bowl for best effect.

THE BATHROOM AND LINEN CUPBOARD

FROM THE UPSTAIRS BATHROOM AND LINEN CUPBOARD WOULD COME THE FRESH AND DELICIOUS SMELLS OF LAVENDER, ORANGE BLOSSOM, JASMINE AND ROSE. SWEET POWDERS AND FLOWER MIXTURES WERE MADE TO SCENT LINENS AND TOWELS AND GENTLE, PERFUMED LOTIONS AND CREAMS WERE PREPARED FOR BATH TIMES. COSMETICS AND SCENTS WERE SIMPLE AND BASED ON HERBS, FLOWERS AND OTHER NATURAL INGREDIENTS BLENDED ACCORDING TO RECIPES HANDED DOWN THROUGH GENERATIONS. LAUNDERING WAS A LONG AND ARDUOUS TASK, BUT THE END RESULT WAS A PILE OF SNOWY LINENS THAT WERE CRISP AND SCENTED.

RIGHT: Sachets of dried lavender and other dried herbs or spices can be placed in drawers and cupboards to leave a gentle scent on clothes and linens. Choose pretty fabrics, and secure tightly with soft ribbons.

SWEET SCENTING POWDER

○   ○   ○

WHAT YOU WILL NEED: *1 Measure Dried Red Rose Petals, 1 Measure Dried Lavender, 1 Measure Dried Jasmine Flowers, ¼ Measure Orrisroot Powder, ¼ Measure Allspice, ¼ Measure Dried Orange Peel, ¼ Measure Whole Cloves, ¼ Measure Sandalwood or Cedar Shavings, ¼ Measure Soft Brown Sugar, 6 to 8 Sticks Cinnamon, Dash of Brandy (optional)*

These days we rely on keeping our clothes and bedding smelling fresh and clean by regular laundering and by storing things, once they are clean, in dry, airy places. In the past, all manner of means were devised to keep musty smells away and to protect stored fabrics from infestation by moths or rodents. Many old-fashioned fabrics made from silk and fine wool could not be washed easily, so sweet powders and flower waters were used liberally to perfume garments.

We are used to the idea of sachets of flower or herb mixtures as perfuming devices, but less commonly seen are these sweet powdered mixtures, which are far more like the old idea they are based on. The filling for the sachets is basically a potpourri of the usual fixatives and spices in a mixture of fragrant herbs and flowers.

Two of the most useful scented flowers are rose and lavender, which are readily available in good quantity, but all kinds of less-common plants and flowers can be used, according to your personal preferences and, possibly, what you grow in your own garden. You could use dried jasmine or orange flowers, both with a Victorian aroma to them, while there is a great choice of scented leaves to add bulk and a slightly different perfume. Many of the scented geraniums dry well and retain a pleasant perfume, as do woodruff, lemon verbena (for a very strong citrus scent), rosemary, thyme and bay. Patchouli leaves or uva-ursi would add a more exotic note. Both can be bought from herbalists' shops. Many other scented ingredients can be included, such as cedar or sandalwood shavings. These deliciously scented woods have the advantage of deterring clothes moths which can still be a problem in country areas. In *Beeton's Book of Household Management*, Mrs Beeton recommends placing pieces of camphor, cedarwood, tobacco leaves and bog myrtle in drawers to preserve clothes from moths.

Many modern potpourris are simply dried botanicals, that is, mixtures of natural materials from plant sources, such as petals, leaves, wood shavings, seed pods, berries, and so on, or even just artificial materials that have been scented with essential oils. Sweet powders, however, rely first and foremost on their ingredients to provide the scent. This can, of course, be boosted with a little essential oil, but a subtle mix of scents and spices is what you should be aiming for, otherwise it would be simpler just to pour a few drops of essential oil on some wadding and put this inside the sachet instead.

The process of grinding and pounding the ingredients into something resembling a powder would have taken many hours' hard, albeit quite pleasant, work, compared with many household tasks, but these days we can speed things up enormously. A

ABOVE: Dried flower petals and sweet-smelling spices are measured out, ready to be made into a scenting powder mixture for linen cupboards and lingerie drawers.

small electric coffee mill does the job perfectly, and although the appliance will not hold very much at a time, the process is so quick that it can be done in a few bursts and mixed together at the end. Every-

thing must be totally dry before grinding it so that you don't end up with a sticky paste. Measure the ingredients listed, using any size of measure that you wish. The recipe given here uses a standard cup measure, but it is up to you how much you make. Try a small amount first to see if the scent is right, then make more or adjust the recipe. Some of the spices can be bought ground if you cannot find them

ABOVE: A small electric coffee mill makes short work of grinding the ingredients finely enough and blending them thoroughly. Do this in several small batches.

ABOVE: When the powder has been ground, carefully spoon it into the small bags and sachets you have waiting, and secure the necks tightly with ribbon.

whole. Just make sure that they are totally fresh.

Reduce all the ingredients to a crumbly powder by grinding them in batches in an electric coffee mill. Put them into a large bowl and stir well to mix everything thoroughly. Add a few drops of brandy, if you are using it, and stir well. Now put spoonfuls of the mixture into little sachets and bags. These must be made from a closely woven fabric, such as fine silk or cotton, so that the powder will not leak

out, but the fabric should be thin enough to let the scent escape. Tie the tops securely if you have used small bags, or sew sachets together so that there are no large gaps for the powder to leak through. The orrisroot powder acts as a fixative, so the scent should remain fresh and strong for many months, if not longer. After they have been in use for a while, give the bags an occasional shake to resettle the contents.

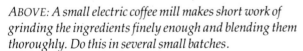

MARIGOLD SKIN TONIC

○　　○　　○

WHAT YOU WILL NEED: *8 fl oz (250 ml) Boiling Water, 6 Tablespoons Fresh or 3 Tablespoons Dried Pot Marigold Petals, 4 Tablespoons of Witch Hazel, 3 Drops of Orange Essential Oil, Small Glass or Plastic Bottle with Stopper or Screw-top lid*

Our great-grandparents appreciated a fine complexion and pretty skin but had to work hard to achieve it. Staying out of the sun must have gone a long way towards keeping the skin young-looking, but simple, homemade recipes played their part, too. While early scientists were just beginning to discover what effect certain materials had on the human body, most ordinary people had already learned, through generations of experiment, that some plants had special properties and very specific uses. In the seventeenth century, fresh marigold flowers were rubbed on wounds to help to heal them. Marigold petals have excellent healing and soothing properties, as well as being astringent and slightly antiseptic. This tonic is good for skin that is inclined to be oily and sensitive skin that is easily irritated. An infusion of marigold flowers also makes a good tisane that is drunk to improve the circulation. Marigolds are an excellent shampoo and hair-rinse ingredient, traditionally used on brown and

BELOW: Assemble all the ingredients and equipment you need before you begin, and be sure to pick the marigolds at the last possible moment before you start making the tonic.

BELOW, left and right: Let the petals infuse until the water is cool, then strain off the liquid and add the other ingredients to the mixture.

reddish hair to highlight the colour. The petals were once dried and stored for use during the winter months. As a flavouring and colourant, they made a very poor substitute for saffron, but, when dry, they kept their bright colour, slightly spicy scent and flavour, and healing properties. Marigolds are versatile plants: as well as their medicinal and cosmetic use, a few petals sprinkled over a salad will enliven it considerably.

Marigolds have been grown in gardens for centuries, having been brought long ago from their native lands in southern Europe, and they were known as a useful pot and medicinal herb in medieval times. They thrive just about anywhere and do not seem to be fussy about the conditions in which they will grow, whether in full sun or partial shade, dry or moist soils.

The marigold is one of the simplest summer annuals to grow and most people can find a small patch of soil, even if it is only in a pot or window-box, to cultivate a few of these brilliant orange blooms. Seed sown in autumn will flower very early the following summer; that sown in early spring will flower from mid-summer onward. The plants are hardy enough to overwinter and will grow bigger if treated this way.

The original bright orange marigold of herb gardens is known as the 'pot marigold' and has fewer petals on each flower than the modern improved strains with their densely packed petals and wide choice of colours, ranging from cream to orange. Try to find pot marigold seed if you can, but otherwise grow any version of *Calendula officinalis*, or buy marigolds from a flower shop when they are in season. Once you have grown marigolds in the garden they will tend to self-seed and appear in odd places ever after. You will soon learn to recognize the new seedlings with their large pale green leaves.

Dried marigold petals can be used successfully wherever fresh petals are specified, (although a smaller quantity will be needed), and these can be bought from a herbalist or you can make your own, by picking the heads when they are just fully open. Pull off the petals and spread them on a wire rack or basket in a warm, airy place until they have dried. Store them in an airtight container in the dark. Because they do not contain preservatives, make up small batches of lotions and tonics so that they are used up quickly, while really fresh.

The recipe for marigold skin tonic could not be simpler to make, and the tonic should be used night and morning after cleansing the skin. Just pat it all over the face with a cosmetic pad or cotton wool. It is preferable, but not imperative, to use bottled spring-water or mineral water for a recipe such as this one, where the water is a main ingredient. This is the basic recipe for making any lotion from an infusion of a flower or leaf, so you could substitute other flowers, such as elder flower or violet, if you choose, and add an essential oil of your choice to scent the tonic.

To make the tonic, you will need a supply of fresh or dried petals. Pull the fresh petals from the flower heads and check that there are no insects among them. Pour the boiling water over the marigold petals in a heat-proof bowl or jug. Stir thoroughly, then leave to infuse until cold, stirring occasionally. Strain the petals from the liquid and discard them. Add the witch hazel and essential oil and stir very thoroughly to disperse the oil. Bottle in a pretty glass bottle and store in the refrigerator.

RIGHT: The finished marigold tonic can be stored in any bottle with a tightly fitting cap or stopper.

ROSE AND OATMEAL SKIN SCRUB

○ . ○ . ○

WHAT YOU WILL NEED: *1 Cup Strongly-scented Dried Rose Petals, 1 Cup Coarse Oatmeal, ½ Cup Chopped Almonds, Screw-top Jar*

The Victorians held the view that cleanliness was next to godliness. By the late Victorian period, running water and roomy baths had become quite commonplace in larger houses, but many people still relied on jugs of hot water being brought to the bedroom and used at a washstand.

Young ladies were expected to have soft, pale, delicate skin. While cosmetics were frowned upon, all kinds of steps were taken in private to achieve the ideal of a porcelain complexion with rosy lips and sparkling eyes. Not even a hint of strong sun was allowed on the face or hands, while the rest of the body was invariably well covered from neck and wrist to ankle. Parasols were carried on summer days to protect the face, and a shady place was always chosen in which to sit outdoors. A dark skin was considered vulgar and coarse, suggesting an outdoor, working life. Homemade recipes and simple ingredients were used to achieve the desired effect on the face and hands. There were some quite extreme recipes for bleaching the skin, to rid it of freckles, for example, but there was nothing in this period to match the horrors of earlier centuries when all kinds of dangerous and poisonous substances were used in the quest for beauty. Flowers, fruit, and vegetables were frequently an important part of the recipes for cosmetics; lemon juice or vinegar added acidity where needed; and the softening qualities of simple ingredients, such as oatmeal, almonds, milk or salt, were wisely made use of.

Oatmeal is a superb ingredient, as it may be used on the most sensitive of skins as a mild abrasive, to soften and smooth the complexion. Take a small handful of this skin scrub, based on oats and roses, and rub it gently onto damp skin in a circular motion. Leave it for a few seconds, then rinse it off carefully. You can also use it to soften and scent a bath by throwing in a large handful as you run the water or by putting scoops of it into small muslin sachets to drop into the water or hang under the tap. (The second way avoids having all the bits floating in the bath.)

To make the scrub, simply combine all the ingredients in a large bowl, mix them well, and then process this in a food processor or a coffee mill until it has a fine texture and the rose petals are chopped quite small. Store the mixture in a screw-top jar.

RIGHT: Stand a bowl of bath scrub in a prominent position beside the tub. Leave a scoop in it to encourage you to cleanse and polish your skin regularly.

HERBAL HAIR RINSE

○   ○   ○

WHAT YOU WILL NEED: *2 pts (1 l) Pure Springwater or Rainwater, 5 Stems Fresh Rosemary, 2 Untreated Limes, 4 oz (150 ml) Cider Vinegar, Muslin, Glass Bottle and Stopper, Extra Rosemary (optional)*

This recipe is made from natural ingredients that are easy to obtain, it smells delicious and leaves hair shining. The Victorians tended to use soap for hair washing. This was strongly alkaline, and so a slightly acidic rinse was used to neutralize the hair. Wherever possible, pure rainwater was used for hair washing, as it was soft and could be collected at no cost.

The difficulties arising from a lack of proper bathrooms meant that hair washing was nowhere near as frequent as it is these days. Today, the showers installed in most households mean that a daily hair wash is normal for many people, whereas in Victorian times a fortnightly wash might have been nearer reality. Men used copious amounts of tonic, brilliantine, macassar oil and pomade on their hair, which probably counteracted any effect washing might have on it, while women's hair was often subjected to complicated hairdressing techniques, involving hot tongs or curling papers, to achieve fashionable ringlets, buns and braids. Women invariably grew their hair long, although it was always arranged in some kind of style and never

LEFT: A classic hair rinse for brunettes, made with the herb rosemary and the refreshing scent and astringency of fresh green lime.

allowed to hang loose. At night, most men and women wore some kind of sleeping cap, which must have played havoc with the hairstyle beneath.

For centuries, a tried-and-trusted herb for the hair has been rosemary. It has always been believed to strengthen hair and stimulate its growth, and it certainly does have an astringent quality that is probably beneficial to the skin of the scalp.

Rosemary has been grown in gardens for as long as it is possible to record. It flowers very early, from February onwards, and the pale, mauve-blue flowers make it an attractive plant to include in any garden. There are upright and sprawling varieties and some with deeper blue flowers. Rosemary prefers a well-drained soil in a sunny position and some shelter from very cold winds. Sprays can be cut regularly for culinary and cosmetic purposes without doing any damage to the plant.

To make the hair rinse, use pure water as a base. Unless you can collect pure rainwater yourself, it is easier to buy natural springwater or mineral water. Bring the water to the boil in a large pan, then peel the limes and pour a few spoonfuls of boiling water over the peel in a jug. Put the rosemary in the pan and simmer for ten minutes. Take the pan off the heat and leave it to cool. Strain the cooled water from the rosemary through muslin and add to the peel. Squeeze the limes and strain the juice into the mixture. Add the cider vinegar. Strain once again through muslin and bottle. Decorate each bottle with a sprig of rosemary if you wish. Use a cupful as a rinse after each hair wash.

FLOWER-SCENTED SACHETS

○ ○ ○

WHAT YOU WILL NEED: *1 Cup Dried Rose Petals, 1 Cup Dried Lavender, 1 Cup Dried Lemon Verbena Leaves, ½ Cup Dried Rose-Scented Geranium Leaves, ½ Cup Dried Chamomile Flowers, ¼ Cup Dried Lemon Peel (chopped finely), ¼ Cup Ground Cinnamon, ¼ Cup Orrisroot Powder, Essential Oils: 4 Drops Rose Geranium, 4 Drops Lavender, Fabric for Sachet Bags, Wadding*

We are all familiar with the idea of scented sachets for drawers and cupboards and perhaps for pillows and cushions, too. They continue to have great appeal, especially when presented tied up with ribbons or decorated with bows, rather like a mysterious gift. If you have even minimal skills with a needle and thread, these little scented sachets make some of the best homemade gifts and they can look far from homemade if you are careful. The trick is to choose good fabrics, perhaps even old ones, and combine these with small scraps of antique lace and beautiful ribbons. Because you are working on such a small scale, the extra cost of this is not very great and the result is exquisite. Use fabrics such as silk, taffeta, dupion, velvets, and satins. Lay old lace over a base of plain-coloured fabric or appliqué lace motifs on to a suitable background.

The shapes you choose to make will probably depend on the materials you have, but you can make square, rectangular, or even round sachets, as well as little bags tied at the neck or cylindrical cushions tied at each end like Christmas crackers. Square sachets look best if they are plump, like fat little cushions, and, in every case, you should try to fill out the shapes to make them look generous and so that the sachet will hold its shape well. Generally, it helps to stuff the sachet with some kind of wadding first and then to add the scented mixture. This gives a good outline and means that you can use less of the precious flower mixture. You can use a natural padding, such as kapok or cotton wadding, or the loose type of polyester wadding normally used for filling larger cushions.

The colours chosen here are a subtle blend of dusky mauves and Parma violet. They seem to have a very Victorian look to them, and the details of ribbons and decorations echo the dress decoration of the period. Stripes and picot edges were both popular in Victorian times, and elegant wide ribbons, plus bows and rosettes, were commonly used to trim dresses and hats. Once you have made a few sachets, you will find that other ideas will come to you as to how to finish off and decorate each one.

To make the mixture for filling the sachets, simply put all the dry ingredients into a large bowl and mix very well. Add the drops of essential oil and stir again. Ideally, the mixture should be stored in loosely closed paper bags in a dark place to cure for a few weeks, but you can use it straightaway if this is not convenient. If the texture of the mixture is too coarse to fit into the smallest sachets, grind it smaller in a food processor or electric coffee mill.

RIGHT: A collection of perfumed sachets and pillows in soft mauve and Parma violet shades. The rich fabrics and lace are complemented by silky ribbons and bows.

VICTORIAN LAVENDER WATER

o   o   o

WHAT YOU WILL NEED: *2 Cups Pure Mineral Water, ¼ Cup Vodka, 10 Drops Pure Lavender Essential Oil, A Few Drops Natural Mauve Colouring (optional), Orrisroot Powder (as fixative)*

Lavender is one of the most useful herbs and is an important ingredient in many different recipes. Apart from its medicinal qualities, it has always been popular simply for its delicate scent, which is both stimulating and soothing. It has always had a faintly old-fashioned image, and has never been considered an exotic or vulgar scent. It is the kind of scent worn by elderly aunts and grandmothers. Lavender essential oil has antiseptic and healing properties, which make its use as a skin-care ingredient logical.

Victorian ladies might dab lavender water on to a handkerchief to cool hot wrists or foreheads on sultry summer days or even sprinkle drops onto delicate underwear and chemises before ironing them. A simple lavender water could be made easily at home, and most gardens had a billowing bush or two of the more scented varieties. Unlike many herbs that require hot, dry summers to produce strong scents and pungent flower oils, lavender thrives well in damper, cooler climates, yet still produces excellent oil. English lavender was always considered the best, even when compared to that

LEFT: Lavender is one of the best known bathroom scents. It is also a useful addition to the medicine cabinet for its healing and antiseptic properties.

grown in quantity in southern France. In Victorian times, fields and fields of it were grown on the south side of London, in the suburbs around Mitcham and Carshalton, now completely covered by houses and streets. Bunches of fresh lavender were sold on the streets of the city and much of the harvest was distilled for use in the perfume industry and to scent soaps and toilet waters. The lavender industry, which reached its heyday in Victorian times, employed many people to grow and harvest the scented crop and to distil the results in vast stills. Lavender scent is at its best when the flowers are fully open. The little flowers eventually fade and drop off, leaving tiny seeds, which we use as 'lavender' to fill sachets and to make potpourri. If picked when just ripe, the stems can be hung in a warm, airy place for the flowers to dry naturally and then can be used for many different purposes. Lavender keeps its scent for a long time naturally and will do so for even longer if it is combined with a fixative of some kind, such as orrisroot powder.

To make a slightly scented lavender water for use in the bath or as a refreshing skin toner, simply infuse fresh lavender flower heads in boiling water, leave to cool, then strain into a bottle. For a more concentrated lavender water, you will need lavender essential oil to provide the fragrance. Simply mix the ingredients listed above, stirring thoroughly for several seconds. Add a very few drops of natural mauve colouring if you wish, then bottle in small containers and keep in a cool, dark place. Splash onto the skin at anytime or add to a warm bath.

STEPHANOTIS WEDDING BOUQUET

○　○　○

WHAT YOU WILL NEED: *White Flowers, such as Roses, Jasmine, Stephanotis, Freesia, Foliage, such as Myrtle, Rosemary, Ivy, Fine Wire, Florist's Tape, Ribbon*

The Victorian period saw the height of the popularity of flowers as personal adornments, and the occasion of a wedding meant the lavish use of them to make bouquets, posies, hair decorations and dress garlands. Many Victorians took the language of flowers seriously, which is why certain flowers were always used at weddings. A vital ingredient was orange blossom, as a symbol of purity. For the bride's bouquet, suitable flowers included white, cream, or possibly the palest lemon tea roses, stephanotis, sweet peas, lilies, orchids, gardenias and carnations, or in spring, tulips, hyacinths or lily of the valley. The contrast of some

green foliage was usually added in the form of fern, ivy, smilax, or rosemary, and a sprig of myrtle. This small-leafed, fragrant evergreen became a vital ingredient for wedding bouquets after Queen Victoria arranged for a sprig from one of her own bushes at Osborne House, on the Isle of Wight, to be included in the bouquet made for Alexandra Caroline Maria of Denmark, who was to marry Victoria's son Albert Edward, the Prince of Wales.

A round Victorian bouquet is quite easy to make. The important first step is to wire and tape all the blooms individually, so that they can be bent into shape and remain fresh. Push a length of fine wire a little way through the base of a flower head. Bend the longer length down the extent of the stem and parallel with it. Twist the short end over the long end to secure it. Wrap the length of the stem (and the long end of wire) with tape, stretching it tight. Do this with all the flowers individually. Thread individual ivy leaves onto wire. Then, starting with a central flower, add flowers and foliage around it, continuing until the bouquet is large enough. Tie the stems together tightly with wire, snip off the ends of the stems and bind them with ribbon to make the bouquet neat.

LEFT: Before putting together the bouquet, be sure to prepare and wire all the flowers you will be using.

RIGHT: The finished cream and green bouquet is sweetly scented and contains some symbolic flowers and foliage such as rosemary, myrtle, roses, jasmine and stephanotis.

COLOGNE WATER

○ ○ ○

WHAT YOU WILL NEED: *Essential Oils, such as Neroli or Petit Grain (15 drops), Bergamot (12 drops), Rosemary (10 drops), Basil (5 drops), 1 Orange, 1 Lemon, 16 fl oz (500 ml) Vodka, 6 Cardamom Seeds, 8 fl oz (250 ml) Distilled Water, Glass Bowl and Stirrer, Filter*

The Victorians adored scents of all kinds, particularly those based on flowers. Eau de cologne was probably the first perfume a young girl would wear since it was light and citrus-scented, and without any of the rich and heady undertones of more exotic concoctions.

The ingredient that gave eau de cologne its special fragrance was neroli oil, a delicious scent collected from the blossom of the bitter orange, *Citrus Aurantium* subsp. *Bergamia*. The flowers produce neroli oil and the leaves produce petit grain oil. Nowadays, neroli oil, like pure rose or jasmine oil, is one of the most expensive oils to buy. Do use it if you can afford to, otherwise substitute with some petit grain oil. This recipe uses fresh citrus peel to add a particularly delicious quality and, because it is difficult to obtain medicinal alcohol these days, it is suggested that you use vodka as a base, since it is pure, unflavoured and colourless.

Peel the orange and lemon (as shown in the photograph) and put the peel into a glass bowl or jug. Add the vodka and stir well. Add the cardamom seeds and then, drop by drop, the essential oils. Stir again for several seconds to distribute the oils thoroughly in the liquid. Cover and leave for 48 hours, stirring again every now and then. Now add the water, mix, and then cover tightly and leave for a week, possibly on a bright windowsill. Shake or stir the mixture every day. Finally, strain the mixture through a double thickness of muslin or a paper coffee filter until it is clear. Bottle and cap tightly.

LEFT AND RIGHT: Old fashioned cologne is a charming and useful addition to the dressing table and making your own is especially satisfying.

FABRIC ROSES

○   ○   ○

WHAT YOU WILL NEED: *Wire-edged Ribbon in Different Colours, Small Artificial Stamens (from cake-decoration suppliers or craft shops), Fine Wire, Scissors, Needle and Thread to Match Ribbon*

The Victorian passion for flowers extended to blooms made from every kind of material that could be coaxed into resembling the real thing. Flowers were moulded from wax, twisted from silk, cut and pressed from paper and assembled from feathers. Tiny, pastel-coloured seashells were glued together to make fragile, pearly blossoms; miniature beads were clustered to make carpets of little flowers on cushions, and velvets and satins were fashioned into full-blown roses that had the sheen and texture of the real thing.

The skilful crafts necessary to produce some of these strange blooms meant that many of the results were framed and hung on a wall, out of reach of prying fingers, or encapsulated in tall glass domes to prevent coal dust from the open fires from spoiling the exquisite creations.

Fashions in dress of the period required much surface decoration. In fact, in many cases it was the additions to a plain dress that made it in vogue. Few people were extravagant, even if they were very wealthy, and clothes were expected to wear out rather than be discarded on a whim of fashion. Hats were resurrected each season with new and modish decorations in the latest colours and styles. Plain and simple hats and clothes were therefore the most useful to own, being infinitely adaptable and

ABOVE: Wire-edged ribbon is the best material for making the roses, but you may use regular ribbon or even strips of fabric. The little wire stamens are pretty, but not essential to the finished blooms.

ABOVE: Wire a small bundle of stamens together and begin to wind the ribbon around them, crimping the bundle tightly at the base of the 'flower'.

ABOVE: Continue winding more ribbon around to create the 'petals', turning back some of the edges to make them look more natural.

making a simple background to show off the latest collection of fabric flowers, ostrich plumes, jet beads, or whatever was up to the minute.

People followed fashion in their own way, copying ideas from colour plates in books and from magazines that circulated among many people in a locality. People in the far-flung provinces, who were at the end of the line for information, tended to be several months behind smart, fashionable, city people, but everyone tried to be as modish as their budget and skills allowed. Most women had a needlecraft skill to fall back on, so they were always able to sew a new flounce or lace trim to a skirt, or a line of neat braid edging on a jacket or bodice.

Hat decorating brought out the creative artist in everyone and much effort went into a new spring bonnet. If affordable, this time of year demanded a new hat, but for many that simply wasn't feasible on a low income with a large family to feed. Instead, an old favourite, embellished with a few well-chosen, or sometimes badly chosen, flowers, fruits, feathers, or veil had to do. Easter Sunday became a fashion parade, with every good seamstress and would-be milliner vying with her nearest rival to produce the most stunning effect. During the Victorian period, no woman or man would leave the house without a hat of some kind, whatever the season or weather.

Every small town could support a draper's shop, well-stocked with haberdashery and all the bits and pieces required to sew clothes at home, as well as a few basic items of ready-made clothing (although nearly everything was handmade – either at home or by local seamstresses and tailors). Wealthy people with large households usually hired women to come to the house one day or so every week, to do mending, darning, simple sewing and the making of garments. A room was kept specially for this purpose, called simply the sewing room. It would have held a store of basic materials, sewing threads and, probably, the everyday cotton fabrics required to make undergarments or nightwear. Such rooms were as light as possible, with a large, solid table to work on. The means for pressing clothes was provided by several heavy flat irons and a hot fire.

Late in the Victorian period the first mechanical sewing machines became available, usually worked by a foot treadle. The seamstress would make any clothes needed for the children, and mend all the linen. Depending on her skill and sense of fashion, she might make garments for the ladies of the house, but often this task was done by a more accomplished dressmaker or, for the very rich, by a couturier. The ladies of the house might do some fine embroidery or Berlin work to fill their time, but would rarely make their own clothes.

The fabric roses shown here are surprisingly quick and easy to make. Each one may come out a little different than the next, which is part of their charm, and if you intend to use them in a group, it is a good idea to make them in slightly different sizes, for a more natural look. You can vary the width of the ribbon or fabric used to make taller or shorter versions, and use different lengths of ribbon to create slim or fat roses. Wire-edged ribbon does make the whole process easier, as it stays where you put it and can be tweaked to make naturalistic folds and creases in the petals. If you cannot find this type of ribbon, buy a stiff, silky fabric that will hold its own weight well, and use long strips in place of ribbon. Do this by cutting the fabric double the width required, folding it together right sides in-

wards, and sewing down the long edge to make a tube. Fold it right side out by attaching a large safety pin to one end and pushing it inside the tube and along to the opposite end. Press the tube flat and use it as ribbon. Always keep the seam edge at the base of the rose.

To create the rose, make a little bundle of stamens, if you are using them. Tie them with some fine wire, then, holding them together, begin to wrap the ribbon around them, but not too tightly. Continue wrapping the ribbon round for a few more turns, gripping it tightly at the base but allowing the top edge to splay out between folds. Pin the base in place and sew a few stitches with the needle and thread to hold it all together. Continue wrapping the ribbon, occasionally twisting, pleating, and bunching it to make it look as natural as possible. Every now and again, sew a few more stitches at the base to hold the new folds and extra ribbon. After one or two attempts you will find that it gets easier and you will develop the confidence to experiment a little.

When you have a rose of the right shape and density, stop winding and cut the ribbon. Fold the raw end of the ribbon down behind the flower to hide it and, finally, stitch the whole thing very securely at the base. Now fold and smooth the top petal edges to look like a natural flower.

Use the finished flowers to decorate shoes, hats, dresses, and evening bags, or as a boutonnière. Attach a small piece of covered milliner's wire, or a short length of florist's wire wrapped with tape, to make a little stem if you are intending to thread it through a buttonhole.

RIGHT: The finished roses can be sewn or pinned to lapels, scarves, and hats and they also look wonderful attached to plain shoes for a party or special occasion.

SPECIAL OCCASION POSIES

○　　○　　○

WHAT YOU WILL NEED:

LILAC AND TRACHELIUM POSY: Flowers, with minimum stem lengths 4 in (10 cm): Red Rose, Mauve Statice, Lilac Pink Ranunculus, Trachelium, Maidenhair Fern, Florist's Wire, Florist's Tape, Ribbon (optional)
NARCISSI AND DAISY POSY: Flowers, with minimum stem lengths 3 in (8 cm): Michaelmas Daisy, Sweet Violets, Scented Narcissi, Forget-Me-Nots, Double Pink Daisies, Aquilegia Leaves, Florist's Wire, Florist's Tape, Ribbon (optional)
VIOLET POSY: Several Small Bunches of Violets with their Leaves, Arum Leaves, Florist's Wire, Paper Doily, Florist's Tape

The posies described here might well have been made for a lady to carry at a special occasion in Victorian times. Women generally carried flowers to functions, whether they were supper parties, balls, or a visit to the theatre or opera. Bridesmaids also carried flowers, often quite colourful arrangements in contrast to the bride's all-white blossoms.

The art of the posy in Victorian times was complicated as flowers were believed to carry hidden messages, so it was important to be aware of this 'language of flowers'. There was an etiquette, too, as to who gave, and who received, posies as gifts. At a wedding, the bridegroom was expected to provide the posies for all the bridesmaids. There was a trend for using posy holders, fashioned from filigree silver, to contain the stems of small posies, and devices to attach a posy to a wrist or waist of a dress, to leave the hands free. Little vases were often shaped to hold a posy once it had been used. The posy itself was usually built up with some damp moss supporting the stems and flower heads and providing a reservoir of moisture – it must have been hard to keep the stems dry enough not to spoil kid gloves. If the posy was very neat and formal, it would require each stem to be wired, which made a neater handle and meant that flowers could be moved into position and would stay there.

The formal posies, with their rings of different-coloured flowers, were as structured and organized as municipal park bedding schemes for summer flower borders.

The posies here are suitable for a present-day bridesmaid at a late-spring wedding. The flowers are arranged in a pattern, but the choice of textures and blooms means that they actually appear quite loose and informal. Favourite Victorian flowers included china-pink double daisies, soft mauve lilacs, violets, and red roses. They do not require wiring of the stems, although the natural stems are wrapped in tape once they are bound together in the bunch. The special florist's tape keeps in moisture. It is unobtrusive and sticks to itself as it is stretched and pressed together. Choose the pale green version for fresh flowers.

LILAC AND TRACHELIUM POSY
To make the lilac posy, start with a red rosebud as the central flower. Surround this with fresh statice in mauve. Tie the stems together at this point and continue building the bunch. Now add pink ranunculus and sprays of lilac alternately around

ABOVE: Two very different posies of fresh flowers made on the same principle. The one on the left includes lilac, ranunculus, statice, and trachelium around a single red rose; the other is a mixture of narcissi, daisies, violets and forget-me-nots. Both are framed with a frill of fresh green foliage, fern, and aquilegia leaves.

ABOVE: A single large posy of the Victorian favourite, violets, made from lots of smaller bunches wrapped in foliage and collared with a lacy white paper doily.

the statice. Tie the stems again. Finish off with a ruff of deep purple trachelium and then a row of soft maidenhair fern. Bind the stem again tightly, from top to bottom, with fine wire and then snip the ends of the stems to the right length. Wrap the stems with tape enclosing them completely.

NARCISSI AND DAISY POSY

This posy is constructed in the same way as the lilac and trachelium posy, but is smaller. The central flower is a small pink Michaelmas Daisy, surroun-

ded by sweet violets. Next comes sweetly scented cream narcissus, a few sprays of forget-me-not and double daisies. A green collar of aquilegia leaves is used to finish the whole thing off. For a special occasion, cover the wrapped stems with a binding of ribbon and complete with a bow.

VIOLET POSY

The Victorian delight in violets knew no bounds. They were another flower sellers' favourite, and were sold on the streets in small bunches with a framing collar of their own leaves, sprigs of ivy or something similar. They are still sold today in very small bunches, with a few leaves surrounding them, although often they are without a scent. Victorian violets did have a scent. There were sweet hedgerow violets from Devon and Cornwall or exotic and rather tender Parma violets bred from Russian and Italian varieties. There were dozens of types to choose from, many with regal names. The scent of violets is strange in that when it is sniffed at for too long, it has the effect of anaesthetizing the nose and the scent appears to vanish.

To make a spectacular large-scale posy of violets in the Victorian fashion, as here, you will need to make up little bunches, complete with leaves, and then put all of these together to make one large bunch. Hold the small bunch of violets in one hand and begin to add leaves all around it, to enclose the flowers completely. The leaves used here were spade-shaped arum leaves that had their sharp-pointed tips trimmed off once they were in place. Tie each little bunch securely, then put them together. Tie the large bunch around its stems to hold it tightly together, then cut the centre from a paper doily and slide the bunch through the hole. Tape or wire this in place.

VALENTINE POSY

○   ○   ○

WHAT YOU WILL NEED: *Dried Red Roses, Dried Dark Red Roses, Dried Purple Achillea, Dried Sea Lavender, Fine Wire, Ribbon (optional)*

Flowers have been dried to preserve them for specific purposes ever since people first discovered that it was possible to do so. The Victorians saw the ornamental possibilities of dried flowers and made them part of their room decorations. As the style of interiors in Victorian times was invariably one of heavy curtains, dark colours and an overcrowded mass of furniture, dried flowers fared better than their fresh counterparts. Fresh flowers were used abundantly at the dining table but less so in living rooms. The fashion for conservatories attached to the house, where people could walk, provided plenty of fresh plants and flowers to satisfy the most ardent botanist.

Artificial and dried flowers were often displayed behind or under glass to protect them and to cut down on the endless dusting and cleaning required in such fussy interiors. They were often treated to make them look frosted and sparkling. This was done by dipping the flowers in a solution of hot water and powdered alum. The flowers were then hung up to dry and arranged under a glass dome. Vases of mixed dried flowers were popular on mantelpieces, where the air grew hot, and in dark

RIGHT: Organize the ingredients you need for the posy, and lay them out to make construction easier. Begin by wiring a ring of roses around a central bloom.

corners of hallways or at the foot of stairs, where there was little light. Dried grasses were extremely popular as a decoration, including monstrously large plumes of pampas grass, which satisfied the common craving for anything foreign and exotic.

The methods of drying things in the past were far more hit and miss than they are today. Plants that air-dried successfully would have been no problem, except during very damp summers, but the only artificial methods of drying would have been with dry sand, or something similar, which was difficult to use and not as efficient as the silica gel and chemicals we have now. Complete flower heads of roses,

peonies, or similar flowers would have been dried in this way to keep them as natural looking and as open as possible. This job is more likely to have been done by the gardener, whose job it was to look after the flower decorations in the house, rather than by one of the indoor servants.

To make this valentine posy of dried flowers, either buy flowers that have already been dried or dry your own. Roses are one of the simplest flowers to dry successfully because they keep their colour and shape well. The ideal place to dry them is above a slow-burning range or cooker that is constantly warm. Ideally, they require a circulating, warm draft of air, but a warm airing cupboard would be suitable, too. Most roses have stems that dry stiff and straight but, once dried, the flower head is at risk of snapping off the stem as you use it. To avoid this, you can wire each bloom before drying. Cut the rose from its stem and push a stiff wire into the base of the rose stem. As the rose dries, the wire will rust firmly into place. A wired flower is often easier to use in arrangements than one with its own stem, as many flower stems become weak and floppy after drying. Hang the roses upside down above the heat source, either singly or in bunches, and leave until totally dry.

All flowers shrink considerably as they dry. The deep plum-coloured achillea flowers dry very easily if simply hung up in bunches in a warm place until crisp. Sea lavender, which is used as a pale edging to the posy, is practically dry upon picking fresh. It is one of several 'everlasting' flowers that develop the texture of dried flowers as they grow. Nonetheless,

LEFT: The finished Valentine posy makes a lovely gift that can be put into a container, hung in a suitable location, or simply left lying on the dressing table.

ABOVE: Make the posy ring by ring with flowers, wiring the stems together occasionally to help keep the whole thing in shape.

it should still be hung up to allow the stems to dry and harden.

This kind of posy can be constructed in exactly the same way as you would a fresh one, or you can use a hot-glue gun to keep everything in position. A dab of glue can help sometimes, even with the fresh method, if a flower head breaks off by accident or needs to be moved into a new position.

The photographs show the posy being put together in the same way as a fresh one, which is quick and easy. Start with the central rose and put a ring of darker red roses around it. Wire around the stems at the top and bottom, then continue to add the achillea, then another ring of roses. Tie wire around the stems again and finally add an edging of sea lavender. Wire around the stems for the last time, to hold the whole thing in place. Attach a ribbon bow if you wish.

DECORATED HAT

○   ○   ○

WHAT YOU WILL NEED: *A Favourite Straw Hat, 3 White Peonies, 2 Red Roses, Florist's Tape, Fine Wire, Needle and Thread*

In Victorian times, the social calendar was governed by a strict round of events, many of them sporting, which followed one after the other through the few fine weeks of summer. Between these were garden parties, croquet tournaments, archery competitions, fêtes, pageants, flower shows and exhibitions, as well as the more private functions of family weddings, christenings, dinners, balls, or a simple tea on the lawn. For those of lesser means, the summer still meant at least an outing to the seaside, a day at the village flower show and fête, a picnic or two in the countryside, or perhaps a stroll to the park to hear a band play in the evening. Most of these events took place outside and a straw hat of some kind was essential, along with parasol and gloves. The few fine weeks of summer were always brief and to be enjoyed at all costs and that meant dressing up for the occasion in a special way to catch the summer mood. This could be as simple a thing as decorating a summer hat with fresh blooms – something rich and wonderful, like full, fat peonies or old-fashioned, scented roses.

Hats seem to be back in fashion these days and not just for the sort of events for which they have always been popular. The summer sun hat is now becoming a necessity, as more and more people take seriously the threats of the thinning ozone layer and skin-damaging sun.

If anything could persuade one to wear a hat, then this shady sun hat decorated with fresh flowers might just do it. It is very quick and easy to put together, and the flowers should last for several hours unless they are under a very strong sun. Roses and peonies flower together in early summer, but any large-scale blooms could replace them just as successfully. Carnations and pinks could be substituted, again mixed with garden roses, or, earlier in the year, try red, pink, or white camellias.

You need flowers that can be cut off quite short under the flower head and that sit flat, facing upward, for the best effect. Cut the stem off each flower, leaving about 1½ in (4 cm) and then bind the stem with florist's tape, twisting and stretching it to cover the whole stem and the cut end. This will help to keep the flower fresh longer. You can wrap the cut end in a little damp paper towelling first, to help it to stay fresh, or, if you can hide it behind a large flower head, use a tiny plastic water vial with a rubber top through which the stem goes. Wire the separate blooms together to make a little spray that curves around the hat where the crown joins the brim. This can then be wired or sewn to the hat. If the straw is loosely woven, it is easy to push fine wire through in a couple of places, to hold the stems steady. With a fabric hat, or very fine straw, just put in a few large stitches with a needle and thread.

RIGHT: This dramatic decoration for a summer straw hat is simply made using fresh blooms of roses and peonies from the garden, pinned in a cluster around the brim.

DRIED FLOWER MIXTURE

○   ○   ○

WHAT YOU WILL NEED: *3 Measures of a Range of Dried Flower Heads and Petals: Including Tulips, Ranunculus, Roses, Peonies, Red Eucalyptus Leaves, 1 Measure of Cedarwood Shavings, ¼ Measure Orrisroot Powder, 5 Drops Rose or Rose Geranium Essential Oil, 5 Drops Cedar Wood Essential Oil, (Use a cup-size measure or adjust to suit you)*

The Victorians had unusual ideas about the effects flowers might have on people. At night, all vases of flowers were removed from bedrooms and put somewhere else until the next day when they could be returned to their original positions. It was believed that flowers had a detrimental effect on the health of the sleeper and gave off unpleasant vapours during the night. Bedroom flowers, where used, were generally chosen for their delicacy and scent, and large-scale arrangements were hardly ever seen. Small bowls of single types of flowers, such as tiny flowering bulbs or lily of the valley, were favoured.

Women spent time in their bedrooms during the day, writing letters, resting and reading but men rarely used them as living rooms in the same way. They had their own dressing rooms, which were more likely to smell of cologne and polish than flowers. These were functional places to dress in and men were unlikely to linger in them for long.

LEFT: Potpourri mixture does not have to be dull. You can make use of large dried flowers and interesting petals, such as tulips, for a brilliant effect.

Victorian women loved potpourri and it was during this period that these scented mixtures came into their own. Special china jars and other devices to display and diffuse the scent became popular and were produced by all the famous china factories of the day. The mixing of various potpourri recipes became a popular pastime. Collecting flowers through the spring and summer was a suitable hobby for girls and women to take up. By now the original function of potpourri had become obscure; it was simply made for the pleasure of doing so and for its ability to scent a room. Most potpourris were kept in lidded jars because they were usually made by the moist method, which did not give a pretty result worth displaying. These days, people usually like to see the colours and textures of the dried flowers and other ingredients and are happy to make potpourris for their looks, first and foremost, and then to add the scent of their choice.

To make this richly coloured version, only large-scale petals and whole flower heads were chosen. The roses have some built-in perfume, but some of the other ingredients, such as tulips, do not. Mix all the flowers and petals in a large bowl and add the drops of essential oil, turning the flowers over and over as you do it. To retain the scent longer, sprinkle in some orrisroot powder and mix it in. This may add a slightly dusty look to the flowers, however, so you may prefer to omit it. Put the mixture in a paper bag with the top folded over and leave it for three weeks in a dark place. Display it in a shallow bowl, laying the most beautiful flowers on top.

THE DRAWING ROOM

THE DRAWING ROOM WAS THE GRANDEST ROOM IN THE VICTORIAN HOUSE, FILLED WITH FURNITURE, FABRICS, ORNAMENTS, AND DECORATIONS. DETAIL WAS PREDOMINANT AND THE INFLUENCES CAME FROM FAR AFIELD. AN EXOTIC PALM IN A CHINESE-INSPIRED POT MIGHT STAND BESIDE A SOLID ENGLISH-OAK CHAIR CUSHIONED IN FRENCH TAPESTRY. THE ROOM WAS A TESTIMONIAL TO THE SKILL OF OLD-FASHIONED CRAFTSMEN, MODERN MACHINERY, AND THE PATIENCE OF THE WOMEN IN THE HOUSEHOLD, WHO STITCHED AND EMBROIDERED, PAINTED AND CUT MORE HOMELY WORKS OF ART AND DECORATION.

RIGHT: The Victorian style was for comfort, with well-upholstered furniture, rich drapes and furnishings. The colours shown here suggest the mood of such a room, filled with velvet, plush, and paisley, and the glow of golden candlelight.

FLOWER SCRAP DECOUPAGE

○   ○   ○

WHAT YOU WILL NEED: *A Small Box or Large Egg-shaped Cardboard Container (Plus Opaque Water-based or Gold Paint if the Surface is Already Patterned), Reproduction Victorian Paper Scraps and/or Colour Images from Magazines, Scissors, Wallpaper Adhesive, Clear Gloss Varnish, Raw Umber-coloured Paint*

The popularity of paper decoupage work reached a high point during the Victorian age. It had been popular since the previous century, but in the Victorian period, ready-made paper cutouts, or 'scraps,' could be bought cheaply in sheets. These were often quite crudely printed, but they had great charm. The subjects depicted were designed to appeal to a mass audience, although some scraps were printed specially for children. Popular subjects were animals, storybook characters, costume fashion, pretty children, birds, and, above all, flowers. Full-blown red and pink roses, posies of violets, clusters of forget-me-nots and lily of the valley were all great favourites.

Many people simply cut out the scraps and arranged them artistically on sheets of paper or in large scrapbooks or 'token' albums, usually combining them with hand-written pieces of poetry or quotations, sentimental rhymes, and little drawings or watercolours. However, there were other methods of using them. For decoupage, layers of

LEFT: A Victorian Easter egg decoupage has pretty mixed colours with a theme of tiny flowers. Hollow cardboard eggs like this one are still available today.

cutout shapes from magazines, for example, were combined with ready-made scraps, glued closely together and layered into a wonderful, rich collage.

Decoupage could be applied to just about anything. Up to as many as 12 coats of varnish or shellac made the surface very tough and durable, so that even large-scale pieces, such as draught screens, could be decorated this way. This thick varnish layer also had the effect of softening the outlines, giving the illusion of a complete painting, rather than a buildup of individual pieces. Papier-mâché objects were considered very suitable as a base for decoupage, as were the lacquer trays or tabletops imported from the Far East in great quantity at this time, which were inexpensive enough to be decorated without the risk of ruining them. In fact, the whole idea of decoupage was originally based on the japanned and lacquered pieces of furniture and other decorative items that had become so fashionable during the eighteenth century and were still popular in Victorian times.

It is possible to buy paper scraps now, but the colour printing is poor, with very few colours used, and the designs are usually whimsical. There are a few companies making reproduction scraps, based on original designs, which are worth looking out for because they have something of the richness of detail and original colouring of the Victorian versions. You can often buy old albums or pages from scrapbooks containing original scraps in good condition, but they are becoming very collectible and therefore expensive.

The best way to re-create the richness of Victorian decoupage is to combine old with new and add images from other sources. Keep colourful seed catalogues, for example, from which to cut pictures of flowers, and store images from colour magazines. Areas of plain colour can be used as backgrounds, to fill in between other cutouts, or as a base on which to glue the most interesting pictures.

The kind of glue you use will depend on the surface to be covered. Ideally you should choose a paste-type glue, which can be brushed onto the back of the scrap and will not damage the surface if some gets onto it by accident. It does not have to be particularly fast drying. Wallpaper adhesive is a good choice and very inexpensive. The Victorians would most probably have mixed up their own paste of flour and water, which is somewhat messy but quite efficient.

There are all kinds of suitable shapes to cover in the decoupage process, from round or square pieces of cardboard or thin plywood to hollow Easter eggs. These cardboard eggs, made in two parts that fit together, are traditional all over Europe. Filled with chocolate eggs and little chicks made from feathers, they have delighted children for years. Covered in less-childish designs, they make very pretty decorations. Old ones can still be found in antique shops, but it is easy enough to create a new one that looks something like an original. Use very small scraps of paper since large bits will not fit snugly around the curves. If you use larger scraps, you will need to cut

them into strips, stopping just before the bottom edge. The scrap can then be glued in place, and the strips will curve over the shape, slightly overlapping each other where necessary. If the card egg you have is already covered with a pattern, paint it all over with opaque, water-based paint to create a plain base, or try gold paint. Cut out tiny flowers and leaves and glue these all over the shell, overlapping them up to make a pleasing design.

Old-fashioned card eggs usually had a small, lacy paper strip on their top inside edges. If you can find something similar, it makes a pretty finishing touch. The inside of the egg was usually lined with a simple, single-colour, patterned paper and the modern ones are often exactly the same. Varnish the entire outside of the egg with a clear, gloss varnish, which has been mixed with a small amount of raw umber paint to give an antiqued finish. Ideally you should build up several thin layers of varnish rather than one thick one. Thin down the first coat or two with a suitable thinning medium. Each coat of varnish must be allowed to dry completely before adding the next, otherwise the finished egg may remain sticky to the touch forever. Leave each half to dry in a warm place with a minimum amount of dust in the air to give a perfect finish. If you prefer a less-shiny finish, use a matte or semi-matte varnish, which will give as much protection but a softer look.

SPATTERWORK LAMPSHADE

○ ○ ○

WHAT YOU WILL NEED: *Dried, Pressed, Scented Geranium Leaves, A Ready-made Nonglossy, Cream/White-coloured Card Shade (Or, If You Wish to Make Your Own, Some Stiff, Non-glossy, Cream/White-coloured Card – Approximately 82 in (32 cm) x 40 in (15.5 cm) for a Standard Candle Shade Stand – Plus Craft Knife), Artist's Water- or Oil-based Paints in Colours of Your Choice or a Selection from the Following: Viridian Green, Ultramarine, Black, White, Raw Umber, Raw Sienna, Chrome Yellow, Old Toothbrush or Similar Small Stiff Brush, Removable Spray Adhesive, Nonflammable Varnish, Paper Plates, Old Newspapers, Paint Thinner*

S patterwork was one of the very many paper- and paint-based pastimes popular during the Victorian period. Using a leaf or something similar as a stencil, spatterwork was a way of decorating a surface by flicking paint over it to create a silhouette

ABOVE: The leaves are temporarily glued to the card, and then paint is spattered on with a small stiff brush. Cover your work surface with paper before you start.

surrounded by fine splashes of paint. By means of a small, stiff brush, several different colours would usually be applied, creating a stippled effect. Used on something like a lampshade, which had light shining through it, the result was both intriguing and extremely attractive. Spatterwork can be done using a ready-made lampshade, but it is easier to do on a homemade shade because the spattering can take place while the card is flat.

LEFT: Very little special equipment is needed to make this small card shade. However, you can buy one ready-made, if you prefer.

The leaves that create the pattern for spatterwork should be dried and pressed flat, and this may take a few days, so prepare them well in advance. Scented geraniums come in many varieties, all with pretty, delicate leaves that are ideal for this design. For a larger-scale shade you might need to find bigger leaves to create the pattern.

This Victorian idea has been used here to decorate a small shade that sits on a special frame and is illuminated by a candle in a candlestick. It could also be scaled up to decorate a much larger lampshade or, indeed, a ready-made shade of any size. The background colour should be pale, such as a cream or off-white, but for a very different effect you could experiment with the technique using dark paint colours spattered onto a coloured background. However, remember that the maximum light will shine through a pale-coloured shade.

The surface of the shade should be suitable for taking the paint, so avoid anything very glossy that might not allow the paint to adhere. Traditionally, oil-based paints were employed, but you can use water-based paints, which are less messy. If you do use water-based paints, you must give the finished shade a transparent coating of nonflammable varnish.

Before you begin, prepare your work area. The paint spatters quite a distance, so you need to build yourself a little surround of card or paper to contain the splashes. Cover the surface with old newspapers, and use paper plates to mix the paint on. Any short-bristled stiff brush is good for spattering;

LEFT: With its delicate filigree pattern, the finished shade glows brilliantly in its soft golden candlelight. Never leave a candle burning unattended.

in fact, an old toothbrush is ideal. Because your finger comes into contact with the bristles, wear plastic gloves if you dislike getting your hands covered in paint.

Because lamps vary in size considerably, it will be simplest to buy a ready-cut card shade, but if you want to try making a shade of your own design, measure out and cut the card in a semicircle, as seen in the picture opposite. (Make a paper pattern first and use that as a template.) Once you have your card shade, lay the pressed leaves on it to make a pleasing design. When you are happy that they look right, lightly fix them to the card with a removable spray adhesive. Mix a deep green with some black in it and perhaps a hint of raw umber and begin to spatter with this colour. It may be wise to experiment on a test piece first. You need to angle the brush and create lots of tiny dots by running the index finger of one hand over the brush surface. Thick paint makes the spots small and light, while thinner paint produces larger dots and blobs. Again you should experiment before you start. You can also vary the size of spatter according to how close the brush is to the card.

When you have found the right paint consistency and brush technique, attempt the real version. You will find it takes time to build up a depth of colour over the whole shade. Now add a different colour such as raw sienna or chrome yellow and continue spattering. Stop before you have a solid colour, so that some cream card still shows through. When the paint is completely dry, peel off the leaves, remove traces of adhesive, and then spatter again lightly over the leaf shapes so that they are not too much in contrast to the rest of the shade. When fully dry, glue the shade to fit on the frame.

DRIED FLOWERS IN A FRAME

○　○　○

WHAT YOU WILL NEED: *Box Frame, Fabric for Back-ground, Hot-glue Gun, Small Basket, Pressed Vine Leaves, Dried Bay Leaves, A Selection of Dried Flowers (such as Roses, Peonies, Hydrangeas), Lichen, Dried Berries or Rose Hips, Varnish (optional), Ribbon*

There was a Victorian craze for making pictures of flowers out of all kinds of different materials, even such unlikely things as feathers and shells. The basket of flowers motif was one of the recurring floral themes used in many different mediums.

It is still possible to buy box frames as antiques or new from a shop that sells picture frames. A hot-glue gun makes putting the basket of flowers together an easy task but, in Victorian times, would have been a long, slow process using a glue pot and needing tweezers to hold things in place while they set. You can position things by eye as you go along or make a trial picture and draw around the outline of the flowers if it helps.

Choose a suitable fabric for the background – one that complements the flowers and is heavy enough to be cut and glued into position without the edges fraying. Wool, tweed, felt, or velvet are all suitable. Measure and cut the background fabric carefully to fit the back of the frame and glue this neatly in place all around the edges. Next, cut the basket in two lengthwise, having first checked that its thickness will fit neatly within the depth of the frame.

Now glue the cut basket in the centre, with its base resting on the bottom inside edge of the frame as the photograph opposite shows.

Now you can begin to build up the picture. The vine leaves should be glued into position first to mark the limits of the picture. Leave a little clear space on the back-ground between the edges of the leaves and the frame. Add the bay leaves, in a fan shape, and a few pieces of hydrangea floret. Now begin to glue the main flowers in place, starting at the bottom of the picture where they touch the basket edge. Let a few hang down over the edge of the basket at the sides. Continue building a pleasing arrangement as you would a fresh-flower design and then add tiny extra details, such as small pieces of lichen and one or two berries to give contrasting colour and to separate the flowers from each other. (A good substitute for lichen is Spanish moss. Although lichen is often sold in craft stores and collected in the wild, it is essentially a non-renewable natural material.)

Try to keep the surface of the flowers lower than the walls of the box frame, otherwise the flowers will be squashed when the glass is in place. If you like the effect, you can spray a light coating of varnish over the flowers to give them a very slight gloss and for protection. When you are happy with the finished result, make a small ribbon bow and glue this to the centre of the basket. Put the glass in place and hang the picture on the wall from a piece of wide ribbon.

RIGHT: Based on a Victorian idea, this box frame filled with dried flowers in a basket works best hung at eye level, allowing the viewer to appreciate its textures.

DECOUPAGE BOX AND POTPOURRI

○   ○   ○

WHAT YOU WILL NEED:

DECOUPAGE BOX: Floral Paper Scraps (Old and New), Adhesive for Paper, Varnish, Burnt Umber Oil Paint, Potpourri, Decorative Bow (optional)
POTPOURRI RECIPE: 1 Cup Dried Deep Red Roses (Whole and Petals), 1 Cup Dried Hibiscus Flowers, 1 Cup Dried Dark Red Tulips, ½ Cup Whole Cinnamon Sticks, ½ Cup Whole Cloves, 6 Tonka Beans (chopped), ¼ Cup Dried Orange Peel, ¼ Cup Orrisroot Powder, ¼ Cup Soft Brown Sugar, 5 Drops Rose or Rose Geranium Essential Oil, 3 Drops Orange Essential Oil

This little decoupage-covered box would make an excellent gift for a birthday or Christmas. The paper scraps used on the box are a mixture of old, original Victorian ones glued over a background of scraps cut from modern day flower and seed catalogues. The catalogues are a marvellous source of printed flowers on paper and, once they are jumbled up, perhaps with a few real scraps, in a decoupage, you do not notice that the flowers are photographed and not drawn. You can buy quite plain, wooden boxes of this kind, ready to be painted or covered in some way, but you could also use a cardboard box, a chocolate box, or whatever you have to hand.

Decoupage was immensely popular in Victorian times when literally acres must have been covered in paper cutout shapes. Decoupage can still be found today, mostly in large-scale forms such as coverings to folding screens, but most of the smaller pieces don't seem to have survived. It can be both practical and decorative if you build up layers of varnish over the paper surface, and this finish is what gives it its special quality. To reproduce that old look in modern decoupage, you will need to age the varnish with burnt umber oil paint.

Make a base all over the box by using the cutout modern scraps from seed catalogues. Choose dark colours where possible and a range of small patterns, with only a few larger blooms such as roses. Glue the larger Victorian scraps over this base, concentrating on the box lid. When the glue has dried, which may take a day or more depending on the glue you use, and the whole surface is completely tight and smooth, paint a thin layer of varnish over the paper-covered surface, using varnish with a tiny touch of burnt umber paint mixed into it. Repeat with a few more layers of varnish, adding a new one only after the previous one has completely dried. Now fill the box with a sweet-smelling potpourri and finish it off with a bow if it is to be a gift.

POTPOURRI RECIPE

Put everything, except the oils, in a large bowl and mix very thoroughly but gently. Add drops of oil, stirring all the time. Put the mixture into large paper bags and store in a dark place for several weeks to cure. Remove and stir. Add more oil if the scent is not strong enough. Use to fill small boxes.

RIGHT: The finished decoupage box can be used to store small items, such as jewellery, or, as shown here, filled with a favourite scented potpourri mixture.

FLOWER-PETAL FRAME

○　○　○

WHAT YOU WILL NEED: *Small Frame and Picture, Deep Pink or Red Dried Rose Heads or a Collection of Dried Rose Petals of Similar Sizes, Pale Mauve Dried Hydrangeas or Dried Hydrangea Petals, Small Pair of Scissors, Hot-glue Gun or Adhesive*

Victorian young ladies spent hours cutting and gluing paper scraps and pressed dried flowers in order to decorate all manner of objects. They often combined a ready-made item with an embellishment of their own design, just as has been done with the little picture in this rose-decorated frame. The coloured print of a famous ballet dancer of the period was probably cut from a journal or book, and then scraps of silk paisley fabric were glued over her dress and finished off with little mother-of-pearl sequins. 'Tinsel pictures', as they were called, were very popular, and all sorts of subjects such as flowers, birds, famous personalities of the time, and even fashion plates, were given this treatment.

This frame is surrounded by rose and hydrangea petals. Use a frame that is wide enough and smooth enough to take the rows of petals; one with a little depth will look more interesting than a perfectly flat one. If it is not the right colour, simply paint it with a semi-matte paint in a dark colour.

Once you have the picture in the frame, prepare the flowers. You may need several complete dried rose heads to collect enough petals of the same size, so spend a little time pulling the flowers apart and sorting the petals into piles according to size. Do the same with the dried hydrangea florets, which will need to be snipped off their clusters with small scissors. Once you have enough of both kinds of petals, begin to glue the hydrangea petals in place as the inner row. Work methodically around the frame, overlapping each petal slightly over the one before and neatly turning at the corners. Now start the outer row of rose petals with their pointed ends facing in towards the picture. Don't attempt to flatten the rose petals if they naturally curl a little – this adds an interesting three-dimensional effect. Again, slightly overlap each one and work around systematically, glueing them into place until the border is complete.

If you grow roses in your garden, dry a few blooms when they are at their best. Pick them on a dry day when they have just opened out from the bud stage. Hang them upside down in a warm, airy place until they are completely dry. Alternatively, you can dry rose petals individually, either outside or in a gas oven overnight, using just the pilot light for heat.

RIGHT: This very plain old ebony picture frame has been transformed by two rows of dried petals in contrasting colours and topped with a rich burgundy bow. Inside is a Victorian tinsel picture of a ballet dancer of the time.

DRIED FLOWER BALL

○   ○   ○

WHAT YOU WILL NEED: *Styrofoam Ball, Dried Flowers (such as Roses, Ranunculus, Helichrysum), Hot-glue Gun, Ribbon, Skewer*

A ball made of flowers is a very traditional idea that originated in the festivals held in springtime to celebrate the renewal of growth. Posies of cowslips and other spring flowers were bunched into a thick ball to toss around among children in now long-forgotten games. A flower ball would have been no surprise to the Victorians.

Many of the fashions for displaying flowers that appeared at this time came from gardeners and nurserymen, and it was in this period that the Wardian case was invented to protect plants in transit, which allowed a massive influx of new varieties into Britain. Inspired by this, the Victorians revived all kinds of unusual and exciting ways to display flowers: special containers were designed, and sometimes dining tables had entire sections removed through which to display grown standard geraniums or exotic palms. One gardener became famous for inventing a stand, known after him as a March stand, which displayed flowers at its base and more flowers higher up, on top of a dish set on a spike. This was intended to avoid the difficulties of dinner guests being unable to see each other across the normal jungle of floral table decorations.

LEFT: This seemingly delicate ball of flowers is in fact quite robust. It is made from dried garden roses in deep shades of amber, pink and red.

Gardeners spent countless hours pushing little flowering bulbs into cone shapes made from moss and wire to present, when in bloom, at the big house. Lily of the valley was forced to flower out of season in mossy constructions built in pyramid and spiral shapes, as if growing in thin air.

The fashion for metalwork during the period saw the manufacture of complicated hanging baskets and holders in which to grow flowers and plants, some of them even planted upside down for a more novel effect. The great conservatories of the period, at places such as Syon Park and, of course, the magnificent Crystal Palace, gave people ideas to copy and introduced them to exotic flowers and ways of training plants into wonderful shapes. The Great Exhibition itself must have caused and inspired all kinds of wonderful notions for displaying flowers. There was a fashion for growing all manner of plants as standard trees on tall, thin stems and another for creating indoor arbours by training ivy to grow over a small sofa.

For making a flower ball, a ready-made foam base designed for dried flowers (such as styrofoam) is required, unless you plan to make a fresh-flower version using a damp foam ball and pushing short flower stems in place all over it. For the dry version, make a hole through the centre of the ball with a skewer and thread a ribbon through this, tying it in a knot at the base if you wish to hang it eventually. Now, using a hot-glue gun, glue the flower heads all over the ball, as close together as possible, until it is completely covered with them.

INDIVIDUAL TABLE POSIES

○ ○ ○

WHAT YOU WILL NEED: *Small Containers, Flowers (such as Freesia, Forget-Me-Nots, London Pride, Cornflower, Lily of the Valley), Taffeta Ribbon*

While Victorian dining tables groaned under the weight of large-scale floral decorations that swept the length of the mahogany, they also found room for smaller more delicate arrangements to delight the individual diner. Tiny posies in miniature vases might be placed before each place setting and a little bunch or spray of flowers left lying on or beside each plate. These could be seen as favours to be worn or mementos of the evening to take away.

The individual place-setting decoration has a use today as it is not only quick and easy to make, even for several guests, but also leaves plenty of room on the table for other things. Apart from this, many people are daunted by the idea of making a proper flower decoration for the centre of the table.

Choose small-scale flowers for the tiny arrangements if you mix them, or use one single, dramatic bloom, such as a lily or rose, in each little container. Here the choice for a spring evening arrangement was scented cream freesias, blue forget-me-nots, pink London pride and a deep blue cornflower. The tiny bunch was made from lily of the valley, forget-me-nots and London pride, tied with a blue taffeta ribbon. For the individual arrangement you will need a collection of small containers, but they do not need to match. Low tumblers or stemmed drinking glasses are suitable, or egg cups or jam jars.

If you are laying the places straight on to a polished wooden surface or any other type of surface without a cloth, then a fresh leaf slipped under each flower container makes a practical and pretty touch. To put together the vase of flowers, begin by putting the forget-me-nots and London pride around the edge, then fill in with freesia. Place one cornflower in the centre.

LEFT: An arrangement of freesia, forget-me-nots and London pride.

RIGHT: Individual ribbon-tied, miniature posies for each place provide a finishing touch.

FLOWER FINGER BOWLS

○   ○   ○

WHAT YOU WILL NEED: *Small Bowls, Lemon Juice, Essential Flower Oils, Orange-flower or Rose Water, Flower Heads*

A formal Victorian meal often consisted of several courses served in a strict order. Breakfast and lunch, while elaborate by modern standards, were much less time-consuming, with few courses and simpler food. When one reads menus from the past, it seems hard to imagine that people were able to eat such a quantity and variety of food at one sitting.

Dinner in a grand house might begin with soup, either thick or a clear consomme. Next there would be a fish course and then an entrée dish of some kind, made up of chicken or other meat. Then a joint of meat would be served, with vegetables and possibly a salad followed by a sorbet to create a break in the meal and cleanse the palate. Next would come the roast, of pheasant or small game birds, or larger game such as hare, venison or something similar. More vegetables might be served as dishes in their own right, but only the 'acceptable' kinds, such as asparagus or sea kale, and certainly every meat or fish dish had its own particular sauce or vegetable accompaniment. Then puddings would be served – invariably a choice of several kinds, ranging from pastries to moulded creams and

LEFT: There are many meals where a finger bowl can be a useful addition to the table. Here it has also become a decorative feature, with floating blossoms.

jellies. Following this came cheese, usually served with celery and a savoury course of something small and very piquant, then on to cream ices, parfaits, and sorbets. The grand finale was a dessert of home-grown fruits, such as peaches, grapes, melons, and pineapples, many out of season; and last, crystallized and glacé fruits, petits fours, nuts and other sweetmeats, followed by coffee.

The etiquette of eating and table manners were important during this period and cutlery was laid out in serried ranks, each piece intended for a certain course. Finger bowls were provided and were generally necessary at some stage in the meal, to refresh fingers made sticky by sweet morsels of juicy fruit or buttered rolls.

A flower or collection of petals floating in the finger bowl was another excuse to decorate the table, and sometimes flower oils were dropped into the bowls to scent them, along with a squeeze of lemon to cleanse the fingers. A large, starched, damask linen napkin was always provided to wipe the mouth and dry the fingers.

Finger bowls can be just as useful to modern diners, and to prepare them, you need to fill three-quarters of small, shallow bowls with cold water and put in a teaspoonful of lemon juice. Add a drop or two of an essential flower oil or, preferably, a spoon-ful of orange-flower or rose water. Now float a flower head or two in the water. Here, the flowers are colour-ful pelargonium blossoms and one or two leaves of a scented variety. The result is pretty enough to look like a table decoration in its own right.

TABLE FLOWER DECORATION

○   ○   ○

WHAT YOU WILL NEED: *Glass Cake Stand, Foam Ring Base, Flowers (such as Pinks, Fuchsias, Clematis, Cornflowers, Geraniums, Pelargoniums, Lavender), Sprays of Red Currants, Currant Leaves, Stemmed Wine Glass*

The Victorians enjoyed their flowers and plants and revelled in the choice and variety that was offered to them, due in most part to the availability of greenhouses to grow plants in and cheap fuel to heat them. This gave people the chance to grow many tender fruits and flowers for the summer months, and to overwinter species such as pelargoniums and fuchsias which would have perished in frosts if left outdoors. Many of the old and easily grown perennial herbaceous plants of the cottage garden were still grown to provide cut flowers, and to fill colourful borders, but now there were exotica, such as gardenias, stephanotis, eucharis and freesia, to pick for vases and table decorations.

A passion for strong colour, however, made sure that the more humble species remained popular alongside their pale and interesting cousins. Candlelight tended to distort natural colours, fading blue away to nothing whilst enhancing reds and golds. Green foliage tended to look darker than it would in daylight, so variegated and silver foliage was much in demand and white and cream flowers stood out. Flowers were carefully arranged in large, flat dishes filled with damp moss or allowed to cascade from elegant trumpet-shaped vases or tiered epergnes. Arrangements often seem to have been designed to show off individual types of flowers rather than to produce a subtle and harmonious mixture of colour and texture.

To create a Victorian tiered container, you will need a flat, glass cake stand with a slight lip, a florist's foam ring base, which can be soaked in water, and a stemmed wine glass to stand in the centre of the ring to hold more flowers.

Soak the foam ring until damp and position it on the cake stand. Cover the ring completely with short flower heads of cornflower, geranium, pinks, and pelargoniums. Tuck in a few stems of red currants. Push a row of currant leaves right under the foam ring. Fill the glass with water and set it in the middle of the ring. Arrange the fuchsias to hang down around the edge, then add clematis, lavender, and pelargoniums. Put one final fuchsia flower in the centre, facing upward.

These colours are very vibrant, but the top tier could also be in a different colour to the bottom ring, to create another effect. The top glass looks prettiest with something that falls over its edges.

RIGHT: This layered centrepiece makes use of strong, deep reds and purples combined with a fresh green border to give your table a dignified look.

IVY NAPKIN RINGS

○   ○   ○

WHAT YOU WILL NEED: *Starched White Napkins, Ivy Strands to Equal the Number of Napkins, 1 Dried or Fresh Red Rose for Each Napkin, Fine Wire (optional), Hot-glue Gun*

In Victorian times the upkeep of table linen must have caused much hard work for the people who had to care for it. We simply toss it into the washing machine or drop it off at the laundry, but in those days there was a long round of steamy coppers, with a fire to stoke beneath, and only soap and soda to get rid of last night's red-wine stains or blackcurrant juice. Drying was a problem unless the weather was kind, and pressing was done with clumsy, heavy flat irons. A large household would have needed several clean changes of table linen a day, and endless napkins would be required for all the family and their constant stream of guests.

The housekeeper would be in charge of providing fresh linen for the dining room and overseeing the laundering, but the butler and other downstairs staff would have to lay the tables and set them out with linen, cutlery, and glasses for every meal. While a smooth damask cloth formed a background

LEFT: This improvized ivy-and-rose napkin ring, tied discreetly with some fine wire, sets off starched linen napkins and gives your table an impressive period touch for very little effort.

to the mass of floral decoration put upon it, the napkins were often folded in wonderfully complicated ways to add to the decorative design of the table. There were plenty of books giving instructions on folding napkins into fantastic shapes, all of which depended on the napkins being as starched as a sheet of card. From pictures of the period, it seems that tables were often decorated with napkins folded in many different ways at one setting.

These days no one really has the time or inclination for such niceties. The simplest presentation usually looks best, so either fold the napkins into squares or rectangles or just roll them neatly from folded squares and place them beside the place settings or on the plates.

For a finishing touch, make something fresh and pretty from natural materials, such as a twist of green ivy and a single red rose. This idea is designed to complement the tablecloth decoration shown on page 110. Roll a length of ivy to make a circle a little bigger than the circumference of the napkin, and twist the ends so that they stay in place. If the ivy has a tendency to unravel, use a tiny piece of wire, as discreetly as possible, to hold it in place. Now glue one single red rose, fresh or dried, in place on the ivy stem. Slide this ivy napkin ring in place over the napkin. This idea can be adapted to suit a special theme or colour scheme. Ivy works beautifully, however, and is generally available, so it does make an excellent choice.

IVY AND ROSE TABLE DECORATION

○   ○   ○

WHAT YOU WILL NEED: *Square White Tablecloth, Dried Bright Red Rosebuds, Fresh or Pressed Ivy Leaves, ½in- (2cm-) Wide White Cotton Tape, Hot-glue Gun, Needle and Thread or Pins*

Ivy was a very versatile material for the Victorian gardener and decorator. It grew profusely in the wild and the more decorative and unusual varieties were suitable for the grandest gardens. Its capacity for growth meant that it was always available in quantity and, of course, being evergreen, it was as glossy and shiny during the winter months as at any other time of year. In fact, it seemed to be in even better condition during cold weather, when its fine tracery of white lines showed up against the deep green leaves. It was an accommodating plant and useful because of the length of its climbing and clinging stems. These could be used for twining around architecture, or swagging across mantel-pieces or the fronts of buffet tables. The plant's neat leaves had a useful way of facing in one direction and were held stiffly and close to the stems.

Ivies could be planted in pots and trained over wire hoops or ball shapes to make fascinating sculp-tures, and they were even planted in small, wedge-shaped tins, hidden behind pictures and mirrors so that the trails of growth would make a living frame. Ivy plants are good-tempered and seem to survive

LEFT: This simple border is just as effective as the huge swathes of greenery commonly strung around Victorian tables. It matches the napkin ring shown on page 108.

happily in very little light and in damp and difficult situations as well as in sun and good soil. There are numerous varieties with enormous leaves, both plain and variegated, some with miniature leaves and lovely markings, some gold- or silver- edged, some spear-shaped and some shorter and squatter.

At Christmastime, Victorian children had a cus-tom of sewing evergreen leaves to banners and ribbons to decorate rooms. This decoration for the edge of a tablecloth would be suitable for a winter party or Christmas Day itself. It is possible to glue the flowers and leaves directly on to fabric with a glue gun, as the blobs of glue will peel off easily when you are tired of the decoration. However, they may leave a slight mark, so it is better to attach the flowers and leaves to cotton tape, which is then pinned or stitched into position. If you decide to use a paper cloth, you can glue right on to it.

Select lots of ivy leaves, all roughly the same size. Cut the stems off the roses, leaving just a short section beneath the bud. Measure the length of tape you will need to go around the edge of the table-cloth. (The cloth shown here is square and designed to be thrown over a larger, circular cloth, thereby forming points at the sides of the table.) Now glue the ivy leaves and roses alternately along the tape, spacing them to suit the size of the tablecloth you have. Make as small a blob of glue as you need to hold the decoration firmly in place. Next attach the tape to the cloth, either with stitches or by pinning, hiding the pins under the ivy leaves. Lay the finished cloth over the larger one.

FRUIT AND FLOWER CENTREPIECE

○   ○   ○

WHAT YOU WILL NEED: *Fruit Stand, 2 Melons, 4 or 5 Apples, 3 Pears, 2 Figs, A Few Cherries, 6 Plums, 2 Bunches of Grapes, 2 Stems of Lilies, 5 Red Roses, A Few Pieces of Leather Fern, Block of Floral Foam, Floral Adhesive Tape, Fine Wire*

The dessert course of a grand meal was the show-place for the skills of the mansion's gardener. By the late Victorian period, a well-run kitchen garden was expected to provide fruits all year round, of a quality fit to be eaten raw. This was no mean feat, but the best estates in Britain could do it. The fruit piled high on dessert stands and compotiers made a statement about the wealth and status of the owner, and diners noted what was offered when they visited friends and gardening rivals for gracious dinners. The table was decorated with flowers and the dessert, which was to stand until the end of the meal. The fruits might be in one splendid arrangement, or certain small fruits, such as strawberries, might be piled in conical shapes on smaller stands. Enormous patience was required to build these elaborate constructions without a fear of them tumbling down from the table. Many hours were needed to sort and select fruits of exactly the same size and colour to use in such edifices, with much fruit discarded for every piece chosen.

Great care was taken to arrange the fruits as exquisitely as possible, placing them in layers on colourful leaves or in a green nest of moss. They were cleaned, but the stems and stalks were left on where necessary, to aid the preparing and eating of the

ABOVE: Tape the foam in place on the dish, and then begin building a firm foundation using the larger pieces of fruit, leaning them against the foam.

RIGHT: Add small bunches of grapes and cherries, using wire, if necessary, to attach them to the dish. Complete by adding the smaller pieces of fruit, and then use the flowers to give some extra height.

fruit. Special knives made from bone were used to cut acidy fruits, and small knives and forks were provided for the eating of peeled, sliced, and cut fruits. If grapes were served, there would be tiny pairs of scissors to snip off small bunches of the fruit. The butler would do any complicated serving, such as paring the rind from a pineapple and cutting slices from it, as well as providing any accompaniments, such as cream.

It was expected that grapes and peaches should be provided more or less right through the year. This could be done by forcing some plants on and

holding others back, but ripening to a perfect stage was often harder to achieve. Pineapples were grown in special pine houses and were a common sight in the grandest homes; melons were commonly grown on the hot-bed system, which produced gentle heat beneath the plants to encourage growth and ripening; while figs, peaches and fruits that were not hardy or used to cold weather were protected by glass or some other means to produce the most delicious flavour. Growing against a warm wall was considered the best way of ensuring that certain fruits produced good flavour, particularly apricots and cherries, which did not respond well to being forced under glass. A few houses had the right conditions to grow truly tropical fruits, such as passion fruit, banana, mango, guava, and mangosteen, but these were still a great rarity.

At the height of this period there was a tremendous choice of fruits all year round. Apples, plums and pears were easier to grow as they demanded no protective greenhouses, but they still needed care in production, harvesting at precisely the right point, and then careful storing. Pears, for example, were always picked underripe, then stored until required. They were then brought into warmer conditions and watched very carefully. Through experience, the gardener could tell when they were at the right degree of ripeness, with the maximum flavour and juice, and they would be sent to the table that day. There were enough apple varieties to provide fruit right throughout the year, by storing the latest-ripening types right through to the early summer and then letting the earliest varieties take over from them once they were ready on the trees.

All the fruit that was sent to the table had to be quite unblemished and of the highest possible quality. This meant that there was always much left over that didn't quite make the grade. The kitchen used quantities of this fruit to make everyday fruit pies and tarts for the servants' meals, whilst soft fruits were made into puddings, ice creams, sauces, syrups and preserves. Nothing was wasted. Hampers of fruits and vegetables were sent by coach or train from their country estates to the town houses of the rich people so that when they were in their city homes, they could still enjoy the bounty of their lavish gardens.

The dessert dish was first and foremost about flavour in Victorian times, but it also had its place as a handsome decoration on the dining table until its fruits were plundered at the end of a meal. This version of a Victorian compotier, piled with fruits, has flowers added to it to make it especially decorative. Of course, the fruits can be eaten, or the whole can be used purely and simply as a flower arrangement and the fruit eaten later. To keep the flowers fresh, place a small block of damp foam in the centre of the arrangement for the flower stems. This also provides a useful, solid shape to lean the fruits against and to pile them on top. Soak the foam until fully wet,

then tape it in the centre of the dish. Begin to put the fruit in place, starting with the larger and heavier items, such as melons, apples and pears, and leaning them against the foam. Fill in small gaps with cherries, plums and figs. Build another layer on the first one. To attach the grapes and allow them to tumble over the dish edge, you will need to wind a small piece of wire around the grape stem. Tie this to the tape in the dish or make use of the handles if there are any on the dish. At this stage, it is sensible to begin to add some of the fern and flowers while you can still see the foam inside the fruit. Cut the flower heads off the lily stems, leaving a shortish length of stem, and push these into the foam, positioning the lilies, roses and fern equally among the pieces of fruit. Continue adding fruit and flowers, to hide the foam completely. Tuck cherries and odd grapes into any small gaps between larger fruits. Give the finished arrangement a light misting of water from a spray bottle and place it on the dining table. It looks very festive and would make a superb decoration for a Christmas meal.

RIGHT: The finished arrangement should look as rich and inviting as a still-life painting. It will keep well for a day or two, unless devoured first!

MENU AND PLACE CARDS

○ ○ ○

WHAT YOU WILL NEED: *Cream Paper and Card (or Ready-made Cards), Paper Doily or Ribbon, Adhesive Tape, Clear Glue (Quick-drying), Sharp Knife, Metal Rule, Scissors, Dried Flowers (Such as Roses, Lily of the Valley and Hydrangea), Hot-glue Gun*

Just occasionally, there are dinners where it seems perfectly appropriate to set a splendid table, with all kinds of little extra touches. For formal dinners, a seating plan is advisable and place cards often necessary; but even if it is just a meal for very good friends, place cards can be fun to make. A menu card, to show off your skills as a cook and menu planner, is a lovely addition to any table. Victorian households would provide these touches as a matter of course. The cards would have been handwritten.

If you do not feel confident about cutting card accurately, try to find ready-made card mounts for the menu card and buy small packs of place cards. Art shops and picture framers sell ready-made card mounts designed for prints and postcards. These will save time and trouble if you are not used to cutting with a rule and sharp knife.

MENU CARD

Mark out a shape for the frame on a piece of card. Cut out the 'window' and then attach a second piece of card, the same size as the first, behind it and hinged at the top with adhesive tape inside. Alternatively, leave the card as a single thickness and simply prop it up against something on the table. Decorate the menu card with two single florets of dried hydrangea at the top corners. Use a quick-drying, clear glue or, preferably, a hot-glue gun, which speeds up the whole process. Now make two small sprays of dried flowers, such as lily of the valley, and attach them to the centre of the bottom of the card to come up and frame the menu slightly. Decorate the centre, where they cross, with another hydrangea floret and a small dried rosebud.

LEFT: The menu card has a delicate bouquet made from dried lily of the valley with a single gilded rose. Use your best handwriting to inscribe the menu.

ABOVE: Place cards may seem old fashioned, but they add a personal touch and are extremely useful when you have a large number of people and a definite seating plan.

Write the menu on a sheet of paper that will fit behind the frame and be visible through the window. Slide the menu between the frame cards and attach it to the back card with sticky tape. If you are using only a single card, tape the menu sheet to the back of the card, being sure the printing is centred in the window.

PLACE CARD

Cut and fold a small rectangle of stiff card in half so that it stands. From behind the card, glue an edging of paper doily or ribbon at the top and bottom. Write the name in your best hand, centring the words. (Do a trial run first on a piece of scrap paper to work out the space the name takes up before attempting the real card.) Glue hydrangea florets at the top and bottom of the card and fix a tiny sprig of lily of the valley to one of the florets. Make as many cards as you need and stand each one at its place setting.

INDEX

○ ○ ○